Post-Modernism and English Literature

Post-Modernism and English Literature

Edited by

M.K. Bhatnagar
M. Rajeshwar

ATLANTIC
PUBLISHERS & DISTRIBUTORS (P) LTD

Published by

ATLANTIC

PUBLISHERS & DISTRIBUTORS (P) LTD

7/22, Ansari Road, Darya Ganj,
New Delhi-110002
Phones : +91-11-40775252, 23273880, 23275880, 23280451
Fax : +91-11-23285873
Web : www.atlanticbooks.com
E-mail : orders@atlanticbooks.com

Branch Office
5, Nallathambi Street, Wallajah Road,
Chennai-600002
Phones : +91-44-64611085, 32413319
E-mail : chennai@atlanticbooks.com

Printed in India at Glorious Printers, A-13, D.S.I.D.C., Jhilmil Industrial Area, Delhi-110095

PREFACE

Literature in general and literary studies in particular have undergone a sea change in the last few decades with Post-modernism. What had earlier been assumed to be gospel-truth now invites skepticism. In such a period of transition, stocktaking of critical postures becomes mandatory. Editing an anthology of scholarly essays covering these aspects has been an educating experience. It is a real pleasure to record my thanks to all the contributors who readily responded to the request by coming out with original articles, covering key authors.

Finally my sincere gratitude to Dr. K.R. Gupta—a fellow academician—whose patient persuasion and irrepressible confidence in me finally saw the assignment through.

I express my deep gratitude to all contributors who have worked hard to write their papers.

M.K. BHATNAGAR

CONTENTS

Preface v

1. Post-modernism—An Introduction 1
—Dr. M.K. Bhatnagar

2. The Genealogy of Post-modernism 7
—Dr. Mohit K. Ray

3. Post-modern Fiction and Iris Murdoch : An Overview 22
—Prof. Urmila Chakraborty

4. Mark Twain and Post-modernism—*A Connecticut Yankee* As Historiographic Metafiction 40
—Dr. A.H. Tak

5. Greene's *The Captain and The Enemy* : A Post-modern Perspective 50
—Dr. Rama Kundu

6. To Be and To Choose : Ken Kesey's *Sometimes a Great Notion* 66
—Ms. P. Shailaja

7. Deconstructing History : A Study of Mahasweta's *Imaginary Maps* 75
—Prof. A. Jaganmohana Chari

8. Possible Stories and Multiple Endings : Rukun Advani's *Beethoven Among the Cows* as an Open-ended Narrative 92
—Dr. K. Damodar Rao

9. Centres and Margins : *Shame's* 'Other' Nation 103
—Dr. Syed Mujeebuddin

10. *The Moor's Last Sigh* : Creativity and Controversy 120
—Dr. Pradeep Trikha

11. Fiction as Philosophy : Subversive Strategies in Shivarama Karanth's *Mookajji's Visions* 127
—Dr. M. Rajeshwar

12. Matriarchal Dominance in Toni Morrison's *Sula* 136
—Dr. (Mrs.) Monika Gupta

1

Post-modernism—An Introduction

DR. M.K. BHATNAGAR
Head
Department of English
Maharshi Duyanand University, Rohtak

The term 'Post-modernist', which has increasingly been in vogue, of late, as a critical tag for a host of contemporary writings, seems an irreverant joke despite its highfalutin critical aura. How can something contemporary and hence modern postdate the modern, being chronologically modern but critically post-modern? The Post-modernist litterateur deliberately goes about violating all expectations as well as confounding this common-sense scepticism. Hence some quintessential elements of the post-modernist body of literature. The most obvious feature in this context is the element of playfulness, amounting more often than not to sheer, audacious, unabashed trickery. At times this results in purposely withholding information or pulling the carpet from dawn under the reader's feet by cheating him of an expected resolution. Who could have anticipated in the days of Fielding or Dickens or even Hardy the offering of alternate endings to the story as is one in *The French Lieutenant's Woman* by John Fowles. Equally unprecedented is the stark *volte-face* that Thomas Pynchon has given to his mystifying *The Crying of Lot 49* where the novel reaches a seemingly inevitable resolution which is most tentalizingly turned away by the author in a wilful manner. Another variant of this post-modernist penchant for pulling, so to say, the reader's leg, one comes, across in William Golding's *Pincher Martin*. Here we do have progression to what would seem a conventional ending but that it is not so is revealed when one discovers to one's chagrin the fact that the ending turns the logic sustaining the novel topsy turvy and necessitates a going back to the beginning again, this time with awareness of this finale. Equally noteworthy is the ostensibly casual and routine manner wherein the supernatural is handled in such writings. No more is one to come across the macabre ghostly stuff tinging the pages red with gore and sending incessant chills down the readers' spine, as in the Gothic Novel, only to be rationalized eventually through the revelation of some human agency. Instead we have a non-naturalized, unexplained, involvement of the supernatural as in Salman Rushdie's *Midnight's Children* where the ghost of the protagonist's grandmother peeps through a hole in the clouds and weeps the monsoon tears as it watches the protagonist's fate.

The post-modernist writers have decisively affected a sea-change in the reader-writer equation which had been hitherto based on the now cliched 'suspension of disbelief' or 'the illusion of reality' going back to the very dawn of the genre. This obviously culminates in increasing manifold the hiatus between the reader and the writer. What must not be lost sight of here is the purposive stance of the writer, *viz.*, rather than feeling apologetic about it or inclined to diminish it, the writer not merely exults in it but shows himself exulting in it. At ideational level, this blitzkrieg on common sense is symptomatic of the vertical split in society in general about the values it ought to live by, the place and role of the individual in it, the worth of society as a unit as such in the ultimate analysis, the existence of God or some other supra-human agency and the credibility of the body of universal truths as well as the very notion of the supposedly general human nature. The only thing certain in such a skeptic scenario seems the disintegration of the concord —howsoever tentative or unstable it might have been earlier—between the reader and the writer along these lines.

Literature, then in the post-modernist context assumes the form of a quintessentially personal, idiosyncratic, even weird vision of life, provoking teasing, confusing, amusing or bewildering the reader in a playful, informal, knowing manner. Rushdie in *Midnight's Children* repeatedly highlights his prerogative as the spinner of the tale and his unquestioned authority to twist it as it suits his fancy, taking liberties even with verifiable, well-known historical facts (*e.g.* the date of Mahatma Gandhi's murder) and refusing to correct the distortion. John Fowles in *The French Lieutenant's Woman* unabashedly dons the mantle of a godly omniscient narrator despite the ubiquitous awareness that the practice is at variance with the general trend of his times. His rationale is : "But I live in the age of Alain Robbe—Grillet and Roland Barthes; if this is a novel, it cannot be a novel in the modern sense of the word". Fowles's authorial stance and his defence of that is extremely illuminating with regard to some key aspects of post-modernism. In the first place, it marks the categorical manner wherein creative writers are inclined to acknowledge their debt to not merely their predecessors[1] in creativity but also in criticism,[2] a practice hitherto unexpected. Much more importantly Fowles here reveals a characteristically post-modern shattering of the fictional illusion. The post-modernist novelist delights in being the creator of his fictional universe and lets go no opportunity to drive home this fact. Equally startling is the precipitate self-consciousness about the act of writing without the least trace of affecting a 'Willing suspension of disbelief'. A novel is in the post-modernistic context a conscious construct with the novelist calling unquestionably and incontrovertibly all the creative shorts. Is it a mere coincidence that the greater penetration of theory in such writings is the cause why 'purist' post-modernism has found America more hospitable than England, given the general resistance to 'theory' in the latter? Not so difficult to explain is the coincidence that the corpus of university professors and practising critics, *e.g.*, Beckett, Iris Murdoch, David Lodge, Saul Bellow, Nabakov, form a big chunk of writing which could legitimately invite the label 'post-modernist'. Consciousness of the craft often percolates down to the genre itself, so self-conscious and purposive is the act of writing along these lines and Joyce's claim that his work would provide employment for future generations of critics and professors is obviously just a secular pointer to the intricate and increasingly theorized and self-conscious nature of such literature.

Post-modernism as a literary phenomenon owes its existence to the cumulative impact of a number of pursuits and disciplines : anthropology, psychology, linguistic philosophy, literary theory, besides others, all keyed up with an awareness of the ideological colouring even in areas of inquiry once thought to be 'neutral' or 'objective', so much so that the post-modernist litterateur is to be seen as a new kind of polymath, having emerged in the eventful post World War II years. The thrust of the post-modernist literary endeavours has been, to use the terminology of the Russian Formalists, to jolt the reader into a fresh awareness of things free from halos or pre-ordained canonization. While 'realist' literature creates a world that the reader recognizes through the use of language as a mediating agent, post-modernist literature defamiliarizes the world facilitating its return to a form where it might be 'seen' rather than merely recognized and this is accomplished in language that draws attention to itself.

Post-modernist fiction emerged at a time when the certainties that underpinned realist fiction had in their turn been undermined. Joyce had striven hard in novels like *Ulysses* and *Finnegans Wake* at creating a form which would accommodate those thought processes and random bits of lived experience which had been relegated to the background, if not totally sidelined, in traditional realist fiction. However the incessant succession of seemingly incredible events during and after the Second World War raised inescapable questions that challenged the supposed universally accepted notions like those of "human nature', 'reality' and 'credibility'. It is against this, background that Brian McHale's expounding of the distinction between 'modernist' and 'post-modernist' fiction makes sense :

> post-modernist fiction differs from modernist fiction just as a poetics dominated by ontological issues differs from one dominated by epistemological issues.[3]

To put it differently, post-modernist texts pose questions about the nature of reality, modernist texts about how we can know a reality whose existence is not ultimately in doubt. Post-modernist fiction in its quest of the 'real' nature of reality often takes recourse to formal subversiveness as the only effective way of communicating a subversive meaning.[4]

The symbiotic interface between the form and substance of fiction, to some extent, determines the tag—realist, modernist or post-modernist'—that can precede it. The term 'post-modernist' is not to be identified with a particular historical moment precisely. The most perceptible difference between the work of Beckett, Lowry and Golding and that of more or less contemporary writers exploring much the same themes is that in the case of the former the stylistic and formal qualities of their work reinforce the bleakness of the content. Form and content in such writings, as in the work of Joyce, for example, exist in a particular relation to each other, forcing the reader to a degree to 'experience' what in realist fiction is 'told' and therefore at a different kind of 'remove'. Such writers, Beckett, Lowry and Golding, for example, offer none of the consolation that a neat and well-rounded form can give to otherwise disturbing material. The content of such material has almost invariably had a generous sprinkling of the unusual, the apocalyptic and even the bizarre. The Marxist critic, Terry Eagleton, draws attention to the unusual perspective brought in by post-modern writers :

> Post-modernism takes something from both modernism and the avant-garde, and in a sense plays one off against the other.

> From modernism proper, post-modernism inherits the fragmentary or schizoid self, but eradicates all critical distance from it, countering this with a poker-faced representation of 'bizarre' experiences which resembles certain avant-garde gestures.

The unbelievable, incredible happenings in recent and remembered history have strained the hitherto neat distinction between the credible and the incredible whereupon the bourgeois realist novel depended. Consequently the late twentieth century has seen in post-modernist writings a revival of the fantastic on an unprecedented scale. The fantastic in the novels of Thomas Pynchon, John Fowles, Iris Murdoch, among others and the almost routine deployment of magical realism in the works of Salman Rushdie, Gabriel Garcia Marquez, Mario Vargas Llosa and Isabel Allende assumes significance in this context. It would not be out of place here to refer to a variety of 'metafictional' techniques in such literature to set off the bizarre and the absurd. These strategies include among others, interruptions into the narrative flow by the writer to remind the reader that this is indeed fiction, an insistence on the unreliability of the narrative voice, lapsing into parallel narratives tangential to the text, blending of the serious and the comic, the sacred and the ludicrous. Such a complex, subtle even unprecedented blend of diverse, hitherto perceived to be incompatible ingredients, makes sense against the current ethos as outlined by Philip Roth :

> the American writer in the middle of the twentieth century has his hands full in trying to understand describe and then makes *credible* much of American reality. It stupefies, it sickens, it infuriates, and finally it is even a kind of embarrassment to one's own meagre imagination. The actuality is continually outdoing our talents, and the culture tosses up figures almost daily that are the envy of any novelist.

Post-modernism meets squarely this challenge through its inculcation of conscious subversiveness. The techniques of post-modernism are subversive of established literary practices and these are often combined with 'outrageous' subject matter. The 'hero' of *Under the Volcano* is none but a drunk whose alcoholism has crippled his insight and sensitivity. Beckett's works almost invariably have tramps and social outcasts as protagonists. *Lolita* is a highly 'outrageous' and morally ambiguous eulogization of the 'love' of a middle-aged man for a pubescent girl. Obviously post-modernism chooses consciously to dabble in experiences and ways of living which deviate in precipitate ways from the mainstream, are marginalized, placed on the cultural, social and moral periphery irrespective of the moral judgements that may emanate from such a choice. The post-structuralist theory involving questioning of hitherto unchallenged and universally acknowledged priorities—that of sanity over madness, of culture over nature, of work over play—has affected post-modernism significantly in this respect. However the post-modernist novelist by making the 'meaning' of his text unstable, through strategies already outlined, renders the post-structuralist reading redundant : the text which refuses to stabilize its own meaning cannot be further destabilized.

The present collection of critical essays takes up for close scrutiny and analysis some key dimensions of post-modernism in relation to individual texts.

The authors taken up cover all the major streams of literature in English—British, American, Commonwealth, Indian. The texts analysed are milestones in the maturity and evolution of these bodies of literature. While even a casual glance at the wide ranging contents would arouse immediate interest, a perusal of the scholarly essays at leisure would bring to light areas of critical interest hitherto left unexplored. Post-modernism offers multiple possibilities for a fresh appraisal of what had been taken always for granted, and the studies presented here are a modest attempt in that direction.

REFERENCES

1. Alain Robbe-Grillet has been since the early 1950s a leading practitioner and apologist of the *nouveau roman.*
2. Roland Barthes (1915-80) was a philosopher and literary theorist. His work encompassed both structuralist and post-structuralist approaches.
3. Brian McHale, *Postmodernist Fiction* (New York : Methuen, 1987), p. xii.
4. It is to Roland Barthes that we can turn for an ideological attack on the formal conventions of realist fiction. In *Writing Degree Zero,* he attacks the use of the preterite tense in realist texts : "The narrative past is...a part of a security system for Belles Letters. Being the image of an order, it is one of those numerous formal facts made between the writer and society for the justification of the former and the serenity of the latter." *Writing Degree Zero,* trans. Annette Lavers and Colin Smith, (New York : Hill & Wang, 1977), p. 46.

2

The Genealogy of Post-modernism

DR. MOHIT K. RAY
Professor of English
Burdwan University, Burdwan

Literary criticism can never be an exact science. Any attempt at a precise definition is bound to speak as much of the time when it is made as of the thing defined. Yet, it is always possible to identify certain distinctive features when a phenomenon assumes the nature of a movement, and attempt a provisional description of the movement. However, before we proceed further it is necessary to bear in mind the semantic differences of the words like 'contemporary' and 'modern'. The word, 'contemporary' is time-based. Anything that happens in our time is contemporary. It is a historic fact. We must however, admit that the word is quite flexible in the sense that by saying 'contemporary poetry' we can mean the poetry of the 90s or the poetry since the 70s, 60s or even since the beginning of the century. We have to define the limits of the contemporary when we discuss something as 'contemporary'. But everything that is contemporary is not necessarily modern. Modernity is a matter of sensibility. To be modern is to be aware of the contemporary scenario as changed by the growth of knowledge; a sensitive perception of the world in the present state of knowledge. The perennial stuff of literature is reality. But the concept of reality is an ongoing process; it keeps on changing with the development of knowledge. We are aware of the huge knowledge explosion during *fin de siècle* and the beginning of the century. In 1895 Lumière brothers invented cinematography and Rontgen discovered X-rays and Marconi invented wireless telegraphy; in 1897 Thomson discovered the electron; in 1898 Curries discovered radium; in 1901 the first wireless communication was established between Europe and America; in 1905 the first motion picture theater was opened in Pittsburgh, and so on, just to mention a few epoch-making events. Let us look at the turn of the century philosophers; Bergson, James, Bradley, Nietzsche and Hulme. They are all concerned with the epistemological issue : the opposition between conceptual abstractions and immediate experience. Their subtle differences notwithstanding all agreed that intellectual formulations are simply practical instruments for arranging the sensory flux in a convenient manner. The spectrum of this idea ranges from Bergson at one end to Nietzsche on the other. Such theories attacked the 19th century positivistic certainties that objective truth either existed at all or could be ascertained through the application of reason and science. Bergson opposed the utilitarian falsifications of reality that we produce through the exercise of our analytical intellect. He called for the development of 'intuition' to restore us to the perception of reality. Nietzsche, on the contrary, regards the experiential flux as a value-neutral meaningless 'chaos of sensations', by no means an identifiable objective reality at all, but rather mere manifestations of the 'will to power' by which life perpetually creates new forms that lack underlying unity with no first cause and no final goal. His response calls for the bold affirmation of life, the proud assertion of our power to lay down new values, new interpretations, new forms that create and sustain a self-authenticating existence. Bergson identifies art with the recovery of immediate experience, Nietzsche identifies it with the creation of new abstractions that impose shape and significance or experience. For William James art is at once invention and discovery. The roots of literary modernism must be traced to the ideas of these philosophers. Then there are others : Darwin, Marx and Freud, for example. The modern writers or the writers who wanted to be modern had to come to terms with a view of human beings emerging from the ideas of these philosophers. The human being popularly conceived as a fallen angel, became after *The Origin of the Species* (1859) a cultured ape. In the popular conception of history, before Marx, the individual effort could play a crucial part. After *Das Kapital* (1867), it had to contend with the possibility that a great deal of it had been responding instead to economic imperatives. If the popular conception of human action, before Freud, had been based upon a possibility of self-knowledge, of presence of mind, *The Interpretation of Dreams* (1900), *The Psychopathology of Everyday Life* (1901) and other works established the disturbing possibility that one could never really know more than the ostensible reasons for such an action. If the popular conception of morality before Nietzsche was of something in essence indisputable, anchored by a concept of a god outside the human machine, and so not subject to the vagaries of mortality, it became, after *Thus Spake Zarathrusta* (1883-85) but a necessary and effective human fiction subject to human readjustment, leading to existential anguish. Briefly, from about the middle of the 19th century the foundations of an earlier understanding of the nature and place of humanity were to shaken that by the end of the century a great many artists and writers throughout the western world had developed a kind of future-shock, a sense that the old view of the world and the meaning of human existence had been taken away from them and that a replacement had not yet arrived, or that sometimes a bewildering array of possible replacements were contending for sovereignty. The broadest view of modernism is that unconsciously as well as consciously, technically as well as thematically, it encompasses not only comprehensions and accommodations, but also the initial apprehensions of this change. The modern sensibility is evinced in a disdainful disregard for authority, a feeling of urgency to break new ground, flirtation with anarchy, temptation to test out chaos and the demonic. It is further evident in a desire to remove all standards, to alter the very nature of language, reorganize our perceptions, and finally stress on the principle of change as an end in itself. The four major preoccupations of modern writers are, according to Bradbury and Mc Farlane are : preoccupation with the complexities of form, preoccupation with the representation of inward states of consciousness, with a sense of the nihilistic disorder behind the ordered surface of life and reality and with the freeing of the narrative art from the dominations of an onerous plot.

It is difficult to find a clear date for the beginning of the movement or movements known as modernism. The movements had been coming in waves along the London-Paris-New York axis for a long time in the 19th century. But we must have a tentative date in terms of literary history. For Frank Kermode thc nineties are the forerunners of modernism; Richard Ellmann would prefer 1900. D.H. Lawrence claimed in *Kangaroo* (1923) that "It was in 1915 that the old world ended". Virginia Woolf insisted in Mr. Bannet and Mrs. Brown (1924) that "On or about December 1910 human nature changed. ...All human relations shifted - those between masters and servants, husbands and wives, parents and children. And when human relations change there is at the same time a change in religion, conduct, politics, and literature." The death of Edward VII and the first post-Impressionist exhibitions were crucidal for Woolf. Harry Levin, however, would like to fix it at 1922, the year of a rich literary harvest : *Ulysses, The Waste Land, Duino*

Elegei Sonnets to Orpheus, Brecht's first play *Baal,* Lawrence's *Aaron's Rod*, Virginia Woolf's *Jacob's Room,* Proust's *Sodom and Gomorrah* and O'Neill's *Anna Christies.*

To confine modernism, or any literary movement for that matter, to a strict period has its dangers. Subjected to the kind of careful reading that Nietzsche recommends in the Preface to *Daybreak* ('slowly, deeply, looking cautiously before and aft, with reservations, with doors open, with delicate eyes and fingers' 1881) almost any text will be found to qualify itself, to divulge antecedents, to share as much of the past as it does of its own movement, and so seem to support the assertion of Paul de Man and many others that much of what at first seems to distinguish a work of one period from a work of another can in fact be found in both, and that the apparent demarcations of literary history may owe less to radical destruction than to failures of close reading. A close reading would possibly reveal that within the rubric of the movement of modernism there are distinct ups and downs. If the 1920s were dominated by radical modernism the 1930s clearly registered a shift in emphasis. Auden, Ishwerwood, Spender, for example, criticized their immediate predecessors for their elitist assumptions and their failure to communicate to a wide audience. With the poets of the 30s realism came back. In the 1940s, again, the emphasis shifted in favour of rendering the refinements of individual sensibility rather than collective experience. Eliot returned with vengeance, as it were, with his poetic drama. In the 1950s the Movement poets, were suspicious of, if not actually hostile to, experimentations. The literary history is never a straight, linear movement; it progresses through a continuous dialogue between the present and the past. What, however, brings all the writers under the canopy of modernism is their serious concern for literature and their religious devotion to the vocation of an artist. De Man indeed chooses to speak not so much of modernism itself as of a modernity that denotes not the one isolable historical period but a series of "incandescent" movements of a desire "to wipe out whatever came earlier in the hope of reaching at last a point that could be called a true present, a point of origin that marks a new departure" (*Blindness and Insight*). Terry Eagleton seems to elaborate the particular quality of such points when he writes of "a sense of one's particularly historical conjuncture as being somehow peculiarly pregnant with crisis and change. ...A portentous, confused yet curiously heightened self-consciousness of one's own historical moment, at once self-doubting and self-congratulatory, anxious and triumphantistic together. ...At one and the same time an arresting and denial of history in the violent shock of the immediate present, from which vantage point all precious developments may be complacently consigned to the aschan of tradition" (*Against the Grain : Selected Essays* 1986). Modernism accordingly might be seen not as the only but as the most recent and most salient of such moments and modernity as a term applicable to several periods of literary history as useful in describing certain Jacoean writers, Donne, Browning and Hopkins, for example. Quinones in his *Mapping Literary Modenism* has tried to map out four phases of literary modernism in terms of Time. The first phase is the rebellion itself against a linear, mechanical time-world deriving from the Renaissance, a time world that in its late-Industrial incarnation empties time itself of all innovative freshness of meaning for its human inhabitants by trapping them in soulless repetitiveness of the production line. Time becomes a commodity. On the experimental level the mechanistic time-world for the modernist author comes to include all the concrete pressures in life toward social conformity, and among them, most intimately, the bond of family represented primarily by the mother. The real problem is to achieve freedom from the mother. Mann, Joyce and Lawrence are examples. Lawrence's major novels, for example end with a striking rejection and defeat of the codes of marriage and continuity, codes of the mother. The second phase of modernism is marked by the development of the complex central consciousness, a new character type that is inward and passive and yet paradoxically, by retreating from willed entanglements with the historical continuum, provides a window outward onto the complex happenings and shiftings of society and shows a remarkable freedom and variety. Major examples are Proust's *Marcel*, Mann's *Hans Castorp*, Joyce's *Bloom*. In the third phase of modernism new meanings are discovered through the appeal of the mythic by which the self is enhanced and even vindicated by its identification with a larger coherence. The fourth and final phase of modernism deals with the return of the sense of historical reality.

Many of the central works of modernism - *The Waste Land, The Cantos, Ulysses* which endeavour to waken from a "nightmare of history", the past, and particularly the literary past, have a high and complex profile within them. Far from ignoring or defying tradition, they attempt to redefine it, to see beyond the formal imperatives of the immediate past and to re-select from the vast body, domestic or otherwise, of the literature which preceded them. Finding their impulse in a creativity highly conscious of its own departure, they must also, as a consequence, constantly remind us the very things which they seek to jettison or modify. Whether we see such a phenomenon as definitive of modernism itself or simply as marking an essential or climatic stage in its development, it would seem that the identity of modernism is better seen as inhering in the nature, range and profile of its dialogue with history than in a clear severance from it.

In fact, in the years before the war many works of literature seem to have been governed by a sense of loss, of personal and cultural displacement. The pursuit of knowledge overreaching itself and resulting in a radical discomfort, an alienation of the human free from its former image itself, is clearly registered in works as diverse as Conrad's *Heart of Darkness* (1902), Wilde's *The Picture of Dorian Gray* (1890), Moore's *Esther Waters* (1894), Wells's *Tono Bungay* (1909), Ford Madox Ford's *The Good Soldier* (1915) and Golding's *Lord of the Flies* (1954) at the end of each of which the central characters having explored beneath the surface of their prior knowledge and experience, find themselves isolated, somehow deprived by their own efforts of the very world they had sought to know or save. In high Modernism, in Eliot and Pound, experience and investigation are seen not as agencies of alienation, but, for those who can withstand the initial disorientation, as the most likely means of restitution or accommodation. *The Waste Land, Ulysses* and the *Cantos* in particular are dominated not by a myth of unwitting destruction, but by one of quest. The protagonist hitherto alienated by investigation, now becomes its agent. Punished for irreverence he or she now learns or re-learns, through arduous experience, lessons which had somehow been disastrously forgotten.

This is why the texts of Joyce, Pound and Eliot are marked by an increasing self-consciousness. The texts break up or dislocate conventional narrative or presentational procedures, sometimes even the sentence and the word, and in so doing not only draw attention to and undermine conventional notions of what a novel or a poem or a drama should be, but attempt to circumvent the intrusion of established discourse upon their presentations, whether or not these are seen by their writers to be presentations of the "real". So each of the chapters of *Ulysses,* for example, employs a different narrative mode and invites the reader to compare the ways in which the material therein is reflected. So the narrative strategy of Eliot in *The Waste Land* endeavours to avoid the connective tissue of conventional discourse and invites the reader to arrange and explain its imagistic fragments in accordance with his or her understanding or ability.

It is perhaps inevitable that the widespread detection and analysis of the systems underlying or even comprising human being should come down to language itself as a system in Ferdnand de Saussure's *Course in General Linguistics* (1916), a theory which would underpin and consolidate this very perception. Saussure's insistence that an element can be explained by its place in a network of relations rather than in a chain of cause and effect partly justified the growing desire to abandon literary history, and autobiographical criticism, and to study literature as "un système qui ne connaît que son ordre propre" - a system with its own order. Since the material of literature is language the structuralists, drawing on the insight of Saussure insisted that literature should be analysed as a self-contained, relational system, with its own rules, a system that does not depend on outside reality for validity. Once the outside reality is derecognized as the authority for literature, the author and the reader are also rejected. If Saussure provided the methodological assumptions of the structuralists Claude Levi-Strauss brought it to the forefront of intellectual activity with the publication of *Structural Anthropology* in 1963.

II

To come to postmodernism is to enter the great Serbonian bog where whole armies have sunk. In the first place the word is semantically anomalous. The prefix "post" means after. Then, how can something which is a contemporary pehnomenon come *after* the present? To say "I am postmodern" would sound like saying "I am dead." But the confusion begins to clear up when a focus our attention on the suffix ISM in postmodernism. Then it seems to refer not so much to a historical time as to a specific movement in culture and criticism. The ISM then would imply that postmodernism is not just a chronological division but an organized system of poetics and aesthetics. Even when the semanic problems are somehow solved the ideational problems remain, because there are different versions of postmodernism. Used first by Toynbee the word was originally used extensively in architecture. But soon it migrated to other areas so as to designate an aesthetic style, a cultural situation, a critical practice and an economic condition. And the problem is further complicated by the fact that the word means different things to different people. For John Barth it is the literature of replenishment, for Charles Newman it is the literature of an inflationary economy, for Jean Francois Lyolard it is a general condition of knowledge in the contemporary informational regime; for Ihab Hassan it is a stage in the road to spiritual unification of human kind.

Harry Levin, Leslie Fiedler, Irving Howe, Terry Eagleton, Douwe Fokkema, Fredric Jameson and others have also used the term in their own ways. The diversity makes one feel that there is not one postmodernism but many, as Lovejoy had remarked about romanticism. But, I believe that it is possible to identity a singular feature - the hallmark of postmodernism - which would suggest a unity in diversity, and bring not only different versions of postmodernism but also postmodernism and poststructuralism into a harmonious whole, or as manifestations of the same basic principle.

But before that let us have a close look at poststructuralism, because poststructuralism and postmodernism are partners in the same paradigm. Together they exercise a joint critique of modernist ideas of order and unity. Both share a profound ontological uncertainty.

Historically poststructuralism had its origin in October 1966 during the symposium on "The Language of Criticism and Sciences of Man" held in John Hopkins Humanities Centre where the objective was to "bring into an active and not uncritical contact leading proponents of structural studies in a wide variety of disciplines." Lucien Goldmann, Todorov, Barthes, Lacan and Derrida, among others, were present. It is here that Derrida presented his now famous "Structure, Sign and Play in the Discourse of the Human Sciences" in which he attacked the traditionalist position in general and the Levi-Strauss version of structuralism in particular. He shows how the structuralist texts like Levi-Strauss's can be made to embarrass their own logic. Derrida contends that the "structurality of structure has always been neutralized or reduced, and this by giving it a center or referring it to a point of presence, a fixed origin." Derrida coins a word "differance" out of two words : "difference" and "deference". The structure of the sign is conditioned by differing and by deferring. "Differance" denotes two actions : differing and deferring. Differing is the one not being the other; it is spatial. Deferring is something delayed or postponed; it is temporal. In other words, the structure of the sign is "differance" which means that a sign is something which is different from another sign, and something that is not fully contained in the sign. Therefore the half of the sign is what it is not and the half of it is what is not there. A sign has no fixed meaning; all that it can do is to send us in search of meaning. The sign, therefore, is a trace and a literary work is a structure of traces. By "decentering" Derrida means that outside discourse there is no fixed point from which one can establish metaphysical boundaries for legitimate signifiers. The critic's desire to find a center is a kind of wishfulfilment and such centering should be summarily dismissed as the useless legacy of the old metaphysics. The idea of decentering has opened up what was supposed to be a closed system of empirical data and the result is free play and indeterminacy. There is such an indeterminacy in any fictional art work that neither consistency nor certainty is possible. The text must be read as slippery, deceptive, unknowable, and most importantly, an unstable narrative. Language lets us down just when we think it meaningful. The meaning is indeterminate. The text is not a closed system but an open one into which we can have access through many different entrances none of which can be claimed as the main one. Each single text, again, is a network that recalls many other texts and opens up the horizon of intertextuality. A text is no longer seen as a veil hiding a meaning, but a web without a centering spider, free play without closure. Once the physical condition of a book is separated from the chain of communication associated with verbal discourse, the book became a simple code that can be interpreted as one interprets hieroglyphics. For Stanley Fish a text is a kind of empty container waiting to be filled with meaning. The reader is the co-author and the text or, more precisely a subtext, emerges out of the vital interaction between the text and the reader. In *S/Z* Roland Barthes uses Balzac's *Sarrasine* as the object of a speculative game and the main interest of Barthes's book lies in his exploration of the other possible stories that can be constructed on the basis of the possible different literal meanings of *Sarrasine.* In the process a traditional fiction is remotivated for the avant-garde. Derrida, Paul de Man, Roland Barthes, J. Hillis Miller and Geoffrey Hartman have managed to create a genuine controversy that involves the traditional historicists, the Chicago neo-Aristotelians, the myth critics and the New Critics. The traditionalists held that historical and critical methods can produce positive knowledge of texts and their environments, provided we accepted three basic premises : (i) that written text says something determinate, (ii) that the determinacy is grounded on authorial intention and (iii) that the properly equipped historian can produce a reading that would be accepted by others as objective. The deconstructionists, on the other hand, argue that positive knowledge is not available because there is no stable ontological ground for it.

Mention should also be made of Jacques Lacan's theory of the role of the mirror stage in a child's development, because of its numerous linguistic and philosophical implications. A child's first experience of seeing himself reflected in the mirror is a momentous experience. It makes him aware of his individual status and enables him to link himself up with the generic man, with other men. Lacan believes that this experience goes a long way in shaping the child's ego, and suggests that it is possibly as distorted as the reflection in the mirror. Applying this idea to literary criticism Lacan contends that there is a text lying just outside the individual's discursive power. The text is that unconsciousness which must be unravelled through language. But what will be discovered are predetermined : childhood memories and obsessive patterns. Michel Foucault looks at a text from another angle and in his writings he has exposed the power of discourse and the discourse of power in his attempt to discover politics of knowledge. Foucault also holds that a selfish interest precedes all power and knowledge and everything is moulded and reshaped to satisfy one's desire and ideals.

The advent of semiotics in the last twenty years really looks like the ultimate in postmodernism. Its isolation of the text, its stress on the self referral, its insistence on scientific models, its use of synchronism and diachronism, its divorce from the signifier, its reliance on the signified, its concern with objects and not the thought behind them have led to a kind of intellectual anarchy. Semiotics has replaced traditional linkage between the author and the book with what Barthes has called a "set of institutional conventions within which the activity of writing can take place."

The deconstructionists, in general, have challenged the stability of a work so vigorously that criticism has lost its proper subject and is plagued by an anarchy of interpretation. There is no reading but only *mis*reading; there is no understanding, but only *mis*understanding. There is no text but only *sub*texts. This denial of any authority of the text has led the critics to fantasize, to write fiction instead of criticism and to spin webs of personal and private associations. For the deconstructionists the work is only a *site*, a cross road of communicative highways linked by external and extra-textual circumstances. The object, however, valuable in itself is just inadequate for them, and in this arena of openended intertextuality we are bound to be caught in a tangled skein. The result is a new situation marked by semiotic volatility and necessary complicity. Thus in postmodernism, modernism's commitment to the autonomy of art has given way to an elaborate intellectual game of remotivation. The most important postmodern feature is indeterminacy. Nothing is certain : we cannot be certain about anything. Heisenberg's principle of uncertainty, Bloom's "anxiety of influence", Man's allegorical reading, Barthes's analysis of *Sarrasine* are functions of the doctrine of indeterminacy. This indeterminacy is also partly due to our sense of fragmentation. The seamless totality of the classical and the Christian worlds are lost to us. With the death of God the world is fragmented; the society is fragmented; the family is fragmented, and the process of fragmentation is an on-going process. In postmodernism this is reflected in the breaking of forms, use of montage and collage and mixing of genres in an unexpected manner. Since postmodern culture is essentially mass culture all canons are discredited. The traditional values are flouted; culture is decanonized. The classic example is Duchamp's presentation of Mona Lisa with a goatee. Art is trivialized and carnivalized. This carnivalization only reflects the comic and/or absurdist ethos of postmodernism. Benjamin believes that all this actually started in the mid-nineteenth century Paris when the first shopping centres were introduced in the Paris arcades. Drawing on industrial revolution France anticipated and promoted what may be called consumerism. While the reactionary movement arising out of the nervous hostility to the democratization of taste led to modernism, the slower but stronger movement spawned mass culture and eventually led to postmodernism. Modernism gave way to the energies of mass culture and a demand for an aesthetics of Kitsch. Postmodernism insisted on the pleasure of the moment, *monokronos hedonis* and looked for things easy to like. The pleasure principle of postmodernism has inevitably led to an endless mixing of genres and media and modes of aesthetic thinking and conceptual art : film and literature, advant-garde and mass culture, the tragic and the comic, the sublime and the ludicrous, interior monologue and magic realism. All kinds of stuff are lumped together into a form which reflects the instinct of *via nuova,* trying to forge a new aesthetics that would correspond to the postmodern situation.

David Lodge identified six narrative strategies generally used in postmodern fiction : Contradiction, Permutation, Discontinuity, Randomness, and the Short Circuit.

The first sentence in the opening paragraph of Alain Robbe-Grillet's *In the Labyrinth* announces that it is raining and the second sentence contradicts the statement and says that the sun is shining. The purpose of the strategy is to disrupt the link between language and reality. A typical example of permutation is provided by the passage in Beckett's *Molloy* where the hero struggles with the problem of distributing and circulating his sucking stones in his four pockets in such a way that he will always suck them in the same sequence. Permutation often leads to discontinuity of text and, also introduces randomness. The loose-leaf novel of B.S. Johnson or Saul Saporta is a typical example of randomness, which the readers can shuffle into different orders. Excess is the device of presenting the reader with more data than he can synthesize and thus resist interpretation. Short circuit takes place when the real, historical author appears on the same plane as his fictitious characters.

We can sum up the postmodern situation with the lines Donne had written in "The Anniversary of the World" (1611) :

> The new philosophy calls all in doubt...
> 'Tis all in pieces, all coherence gone,
> All just supply and all relation...
> For every man alone thinks he hath got
> To be a phoenix, and that then can be
> None of that kind, of which he is, but he.

III

It is now time we considered some of the basic differences between modernism and postmodernism. Modernism cultivated austerity; postmodernism is interested in pleasure. Modernism tried to capture reality through individual consciousness which was equivalent of life itself. Virginia Woolf saw life as a "semitransparent envelope", "a luminous halo". Eliot's objective correlative, Joyce's epiphany and the imagist doctrine offer glimpses of reality. Modernism believed that there is a centre and, in the words of Henry James "a pattern in the carpet". Myth and musical form were often used to give a structured unity to a chaotic material. For postmodernism "realism" is just an incoherent and deluding notion. Against the modernist's struggle for wholeness and unity postmodernism posits a radical indeterminacy. For postmodernism the pattern, or the centre is only a wishful thinking; an imposition. The idea of a meaningful pattern is a comforting fiction at the best. No amount of research can, for example, establish the identity of the man with the heavy coat and hat and stick encountered by Moran in Beckett's *Molloy*. It is impossible to comprehend the plot of John Fowles' *The Magus* or Thomas Pynchon's *The Crying of Lot 49*. These novels are more concerned with ontological rather than epistemological issues. One way to understand the contrastive features of modernism and postmodernism is with the help of a table.

Modernism	*Postmodernism*
Form	Antiform/disjunctive/open

Purpose	Play
Design	Chance
Art Object	Process
Distance	Participation
Creation/Synthesis	Deconstruction/Antithesis
Presence	Absence
Determinacy	Indeterminacy

IV

Although it may appear that postmodernism has completely broken away from modernism in a radical way, it is however, possible, at least in case of postmodernism in criticism, to trace some of its basic ideas to earlier periods of literary history. Stern's *Tristram Shandy* written in the 1760s can be seen as a postmodern novel in the sense it is a self-reflexive and self-conscious novel the substance of which consists in defining its own structure. In this century Andre Gide's *Les Faux Monnayeurs* (1927) provides another example of self-reflexive novel. Again, if unknowability is one of the major aspects of postmodernism, it is abundantly evident in Camus's *The Fall* and *The Outsider*. In Camus, there is no centre, no fixedness outside the discourse itself, and even that is vague, uncertain, indeterminate. When the deconstructionists stress the fact that language always betrays us at the moment when we most seek certainty or stability from it, they are only calling attention to an aspect of communication that has been a major concern of Kandinsky in his earliest phase, of Pound in *The Cantos,* of Eliot in *The Waste Land* and Rilke in *Duino Elegies,* just to name a few. If Derrida insists that there can be no real division between fiction and nonfiction, that is exactly what Rimbaud in his letters to Demeny (1871) and in his poem "Le bateau ivre" (The Drunken Boat) was trying to suggest. The idea of redirection effected by the notion of reader as coauthor can be traced to Baudelaire (hypocrite lecteur : mon semblable, mon frère) and Kafka. Kafka's *The Castle* forces a constant realignment of text and reader through irony, tone and decentering. Even Baudelaire's voyage-images are multi-levelled in their educative power : the voyage is a kind of a linkage between the artist and the reader. Lacan's mirror-image theory reminds one of Mallarmé. In *Herodiade* and many other poems, notably in "Un Dentelle s'abolit" the mirror is the window with which the lace curtain interacts, and this interaction produces an unconscious language leading to creativity, as the mirror works with the reflections of meaning which lie in the unconscious. Mallarmé also anticipates postmodernism in his use of breaks and blanks by which he internalizes intertextual heterogeneity and puts it to work not as relation between texts but as a play of intervals and interruptions within texts. Mallarmé's intertextuality thus becomes an explicit version of the ways in which a text is never its own contemporary, cannot constitute a self-contained whole, conveys only its non-coincidence with itself. In Camus's *The Fall* there is no centre, no totality, no certainty. There is only delay, spacing, temporalizing and displacement.

V

Even then there is no reason to think that postmodernism is the last word in culture and criticism. The facts falsify the situation supposedly created by postmodernism. Serious scholars, teachers and researchers all over the world are seriously engaged in interpreting, annotating, explicating and editing texts. They are engaged in the common pursuit of knowledge in their search for sources and biographical facts, in their study of the social and historical background, in everything, in fact, that can help us to understand and enjoy the energy dynamics of a literary discourse.

SELECT BIBLIOGRAPHY

Benjamin, Walter, "The Work of Art in the Age of Mechanical Reproduction" *Illuminations*, Trans. Harry Zohn, New York : Schochken, 1969. The easy was first published in 1935.

Bradbury, Malcolm and James McFarlane, eds. *Modernism*, London : Penguin Books, 1976.

Brooker, Peter, ed. *Modernism/Postmodernism*, London : Longman, 1992.

Buchbinder, David, *Contemporary Literary Theory and the Reading of Poetry*, South Melbourne : Macmillan Education Australia Pvt. Ltd., 1991.

Calinescu, Matei, *Five Faces of Modernity : Modernism, Avant-Garde, Decadence, Kitsch, Postmodernism*, Durham : Duke University Press, 1987.

Cohen, Ralph, *Future Literary Theory*, New York : Routledge, 1989.

Falck, Colin, *Myth, Truth and Literature : Towards a true post-modernism* Cambridge : Cambridge University Press, 1989.

Fokkema, Douwe and Hans Birtens eds., *Approaching Postmodernism*, Amsterdom : John Benjamins, 1986.

Hassan, Ihab Sally Hassan, eds., *Innovation/Renovation : New Perspectives on the Humanities*, Madison : University of Wisconsin Press, 1983.

Hutcheon, Linda, *A Poetics of Postmodernism*, London : Routledge, 1988.

Karl, Frederick R., *Modern and Modernism : The Sovereignty of the Artist 1885-1925*, New York : Atheneum, 1985.

Lentricchia, Frank, *After the New Criticism,* Chicago : University of Chicago Press, 1980.

Levenson, Michael H., *A Genealogy of Modernism : A Study of English Literary Doctrine 1908-1922,* Cambridge : Cambridge University Press, 1984.

Lodge, David, *Working with Structuralism*, Boston : Routledge and Kegan Paul, 1981.

McHale, Brian, *Postmodernist Fiction,* London : Routledge, 1987.

Norris, Christopher, *Deconstruction : Theory and Practice,* London : Methuen, 1982.

Quinones, Ricardo J., *Mapping Literary Modernism : Time and Development*, Princeton : Princeton University Press, 1985.

Schwartz, Sanford, *The Matrix of Modernism : Pound, Eliot, and Early Twentieth Century Thought*, Princeton : Princeton University Press, 1985.

Sharatt, Bernard, "Eliot : Modernism, Postmodernism, and after," The *Cambridge Companion to T.S. Eliot*, Ed. A.D. Moody, Cambridge : Cambridge University Press, 1994.

3

Post-modern Fiction and Iris Murdoch : An Overview

PROF. URMILA CHAKRABORTY
Head
Department of English
University of North Bengal, West Bengal

In *The Future of the Novel*, Henry James wrote,

> "It has arrived, in truth, the novel, late at self-consciousness; but it has done its utmost ever since to make up for lost opportunities."[1]

James was writing in 1899, and he already saw a split growing between the popular and the aesthetic functions of the novel. He envisaged new directions, new possibilities for the novel form, and indeed upto the twenties and the thirties, the novel realized its poetic and symbolist potential. This was the age of modernism when the novel veered off from the realistic mode of nineteenth century fiction, and turned inward. Along with an exploration of the symbolic and mythic resources of the novel came bold experiments in the novel form and an exploration of the flow of individual consciousness.

Actually, the realistic novel died a natural death because of certain historicist reasons. The novel in the nineteenth century was the product of a social order and a world view that had been irretrievably lost. It depended on a shared communal language through which people could interchange their esperiences and interpretations of the world, their structures of value and perceptions of reality. The twentieth century saw the disappearance of this shared language because of the breakdown of the familiar ordered society. The nineteenth century novel projected the image of the rounded, individuated, private self, a recognizable being with whom the reader could identify. The twentieth century view of man was at odds with this conception, seeing man as the alienated fragmented consciousness that he is. Further, the novelists looked upon the well made plot, or story on which the realistic novel depended as something that had been forcibly imposed upon the familiar anarchy of experience.

The modernist novel tried to come to terms with the altered perspective on life by questioning all the givens of earlier fiction. Eschewing the comson currency of language, the common understanding of history, the shared sense of a structured and ordered society, it moved in two directions. Either it turned inward, trying to capture psychic states and the constant flux of the human consciousness, or it tended to project the futility and anarchy of modern life in a mythic mode. But essentially the modern novel moved away from realism and humanized representation, and concentrated more on form. In *The Dehumanization of Art* Ortega Y. Gasset complained that because of its shift away from realism, the modern novel tended to become a game or a delightful fraud. It stressed the power of form and technique, on the musicalities of composition, appealing to the reader's sense of aesthetic harmony, and the sense of the existence of a difficult divergence between art and reality.

The implications of the modernist view of the novel are still with us, but in some ways modernism more or less exhausted experiment, and made it difficult for the post-modern writer to establish a new aesthetic environment. Moreover, the need for an aesthetic revolt against environmental realism or Victorian sentimentality being no longer important, the need for literary revolutionism was less sharp in the forties. The historical situation altered with the Second World War. We were moving in a new kind of world in which a different order of human experience was present and the war had totally broken down any residual faith in an ordered world or in the progress of human civilization. New ideas and ideologies were becoming active in a world of shattered beliefs. The devastation of war, the collapse of values, the genocide in Germany, the rise of totalitarian systems—so much had happened between the two wars. The years during and after the second world war were the years when the day to day battle for mere subsistence made all essentialist values appear absurd, and existentialism was born. It was hardly probable that the novelist would be content to engage himself/herself in facile formal experiments. Instead, there appeared in fiction an angry social realism. In the inchoate society that was born after the war the novelist was turning away both from modernist symbolism and formalism and earlier humanistic moralism. He was engaged, in various ways, in complex explorations between the world of form and the world of history, of cultural upheavals and class relations. Thus, in the postwar years, realism and experiment, as Malcolm Bradbury says, came

> "oddly close together, giving us, among other things, a realism almost surrealist because it so much distrusted the constituents of reality, and a formalism that was obsessively concerned with documentation. In brief, there was a considerable blurring of old categories, and, slowly emerging, a new debate about the status of fiction, as well as a fresh and lively phase in literature."[2]

In England the dominant mood of postwar fiction was that of anger, and this anger was directed not only against modernism but against Bloomsbury and a particular literary and cultural milieu with decided class associations. In the fifties was born The Movement, and when Iris Murdoch's first novel, *Under the Net* was published in 1954 it was hailed as a Movement work. The Movement was really a reaction, in poetry and literature, against the "haut-bourgeois" generation of the thirties, and was, therefore, looked down upon by the earlier generation. Stephen Spender called them "Lower Middle Brows" and Edith Sitwell spoke of their "lifeless quatrains". Movement texts often included deprecating or obscene references to culture, was prejudiced against the culture of abroad and described a landscape that usually bore the marks of industry and also of class divisions exacerbated by the industrialisation process. The key figures in Movement fiction were Kingsley Amis and John Wain, and they created a new type of hero who connected Movement fiction to current social change. The new postwar fictional type was described by A. Alvarez as

> "the postwar Welfare State Englishman : shabby and not concerned with his appearance; poor, he has a bike, not a car; underfed, underpaid, overtaxed, hopeless, bored, wry."[3]

At the same time upward social mobility is a recurrent theme of Movement work, and it often determines narrative structure. Wain's *Hurry on Down* and Amis' *Lucky Jim* and *That Uncertain Feeling* are concerned with the struggle of a male protagonist to adjust to the values of another class. There are certain features that are typical of the Movement novel. Very often a hero from the working or lower middle class or even middle-middle-class, is thrust into an upper-middle-class milieu through some acquaintance with a member of that class. He meets a heroine of a higher social standing, and either attains her

(*Lucky Jim, Hurry on Down*) and gets a better job or withdraws back to his original social status (*That Uncertain Feeling*). Even though the Movement writers disclaimed any class-consciousness or responsiveness to any social change, their insights into the class question made their readers accept their fiction as the literature of the age, "the only zeitgeist literature we have".[4]

This angry social realism is represented by significant writers like Amis, Wain, Sillitoe, and David Storey. But there is in contemporary fiction another more visionary and "fantastic" manner influenced mainly by the novels of Beckett. In his novels realistic landscape disappears as words tend to become objects in their own right and the author's power to form patterns with them becomes symbolical of the relationship between the individual and the environment. The influence of Beckett on Iris Murdoch was immense, and Malcolm Bradbury writes,

> "Her first book *Under the Net* (1954) was brought under the net of anger; in fact it was the first of a long and developing sequence of symbolist-philosophical novels dealing with the problems of language, meaning and myth-making, and concerned with a kind of structuralist anthropological view of the root-forces that live through and behind society—love, power, totemism, force".[5]

Actually, Murdoch, in some respects, did belong to the Movement generation. She knew John Wain, had been an undergraduate in Oxford from 1939 to 1942, and was a teacher there from 1948 onwards. *Under the Net* shows unmistakable similarities with Movement novels. The picaresque structure of the novel invited comparisons with Amis' *Lucky Jim*. The city scapes bear the marks of the industrialisation process, and here is a typical description :

> "On either side the walls of the warehouses jutted out , cutting our view and sheltering the inlet where the river came to us thick with scum and floating spars of wood, full to overflowing in the bosom of London."[6]

Moreover, the restless and rebellious hero Jake Donaghue is the typical hero of the Movement generation. He has no money, no social position, no fixed dwelling, and yet he is acutely conscious of his petit-bourgeois class values. When Sammy wants to give him money to keep him off from Magdalm, it dawns upon him that he is being bought off and even though he is literally penniless, he tells Sammy that he can't possibly take money, because, as he says :

> "I don't belong to a social class that takes money in a situation like this."[7]

But given her background, Iris Murdoch could hardly be respected to remain content to describe contemporary social reality. She was born in Dublin in 1919 of Anglo-Irish parents. Even though she was brought up in London, she used to spend holidays in Ireland, a place she looked upon as "a very romantic land, a land I wanted to get to and discover".[8] Her Anglo-lrish lineage and this constant link with Ireland possibly generated in her the sense of being an outsider, and she commented to Haffenden :

> "I feel as I grow older that we were wanderers, and I've only recently realised that I'm a kind of exile, a displaced person. I identify with exiles."[9]

Combined with this sense of being an exile was her sense of loneliness. She was an only child, and in her interview at Caen, she connected her writing drive to a search for brothers and sisters. In this she sees a reason for her own and Sartre's fascination with twins. The relationship she depicts between Hilary Burde and his sister Crystal in her late novel *The Word Child* shows how poignant this theme remains for her to the end.

She studied ancient history, classics and philosophy at Sommerville College, Oxford. From 1942 to 1944 she worked as a temporary wartime civil servant, and then for the following two years worked with the United Nations Relief and Rehabilitation Administration, first in Belgium, then in Austria, where she worked in a camp for displaced persons. It was this exposure to postwar Europe which was responsible for her liberation from the comparative insularity of much of postwar British fiction. It helped to widen her horizons, her area of perception. Whereas Movement literature was very much against the culture of abroad[10], Murdoch kept herself open to the cultural and philosophical climate of postwar Europe. In her interview with Haffenden she said that she saw a "total breakdown of human society" which she considered to be instructive. Peter J. Conradi comments :

> "This breakdown of society produced refugees and homeless persons who figure in Murdoch's novels, as in history, and Sartrean existentialism was a philosophy that privileged the cultureless outsider hero."[11]

Iris Murdoch is one of those rare people who have excelled as philosophers as well as novelists, and it is significant that in her first published book she writes on a philosopher novelist; *Sartre* : *Romantic*

Rationalist, 1953. She wrote a number of philosophical treatises including "Existentialists and Mystics". "The Sublime and the Good", and "Against Dryness", and in 1977 published her book on Platonic philosophy, *The Fire and the Sun : Why Plato Banished the Artists*.

In *Sartre : Romantic Rationalist* she appears to attach great value to the importance that existentialist philosophy gave to experience. This was something new, something that was the gift of the excruciating experience of the war and the realization of

> "the amazing inadequacy of man, the ease with which he can be made to submit to thc unnatural and thc frightful, simply because, as a rule, he prizes the routine of ordinary existence above everything else."[12]

But her sceptical attitude to the existentialist picture of man is clearly apparent from the very first. She does not accept either self-knowledge or sincerity as acceptable as primary virtues, and for her man is not innately rational, good, or free. We have to struggle continuously to earn reason, and thus to be free. She argues that there is in existentialism an over-emphasis on the will. It opposes, too simply, an innocent self to a guilty society. It separates the moral agent from all that surrounds him. Ignoring the daunting power of the secret fragmentary opaque and obsessive inner life of the personality, it assumes that the will could be free. In her essay "Existentialists and Mystics" in 1970 she attacked the hero of much contemporary fiction as :

> "the lonely brave man, defiant without optimism, proud without pretension, always an exposer of shams, whose mode of being is a deep criticism of society. He is an adventurer. He is godless. He does not suffer from guilt. He thinks of himself as free. He may have faults, he may be self-assertive, or even violent, but he has sincerity and courage, and for this we forgive him. ... He *might* do anything."

Murdoch calls this hero existentialist, and sees in him an inheritance from Romanticism. She notes that this hero, whom we find in the novels of Hemingway, Lawrence, Sartre, Camus, Amis, is already a little out of date. In an interview she said that it is typical of existentialism that it

> "either makes his responsibility absolute or abolishes it."[13]

As Peter J. Conradi puts it, for Murdoch,

> "Existentialism's promise of total human freedom is a bogus one. Much of Murdoch's moral psychology boils down to a criticism of fast moral change as romantic and false, and a

> defence of slow moral change as something difficult, piece-meal, and always incomplete."[14]

In her book on Sartre she is much concerned with limiting and defining his notions of freedom both in art and politics. In her article "The Sublime and the Beautiful Revisited" she relates freedom to virtue, and both are related to beauty too, because they are related to the kind of formal truth-seeking of the artist.

> "Virtue is not essentially or immediately concerned with choosing between actions or rules or reasons nor with stripping the personality for a leap. It is concerned with really apprehending that other people exist. This, too, is what freedom actually is, and it is almost impossible not to feel the creation of a work of art as a struggle for freedom.... Freedom is knowing and understanding and respecting things quite other than ourselves."[15]

Murdoch connects this concept of virtue with a term she learns from Simone Weil, "attention". Attention, for Weil, means a constantly renewed attempt to see things, objects, people, moral situations, truly as they are, untainted by subjective colouring. This willed, thoughtful, selfless contemplation enables people to make moral decisions in terms of this attention. Influenced by Weil's concept, Murdoch writes,

> "Freedom is not strictly the exercise of the will, but rather the experience of accurate vision which, when this becomes appropriate, occasions action."[16]

Murdoch is really a moral philosopher who connects this concept of attention to the concept of good, or goodness. She believes that this attention will bring us to the point of goodness and truth. (Weil : God)

As a philosopher and a novelist Murdoch is mainly concerned with two things. She returns again and again to the particularity of things and individuals, warning us against simplified theories. A crucial word with her is "contingency" which is used to describe what is random and accidental about people, not part of any formal plan. She misses in the philosopher novelist Sartre

> "the apprehension of the absurd irreducible uniqueness of people and of their relations with each other."[17]

The other problem is one which Beckett has struggled with, and which is one of the most crucial ones for the novelist. In a conversation with Malcolm Bradbury in 1976 Murdoch described her novels as pilgrimages from illusion towards reality, and also pointed out that 'reality' as such is never arrived at either in life or in books which depend on language as a medium. Her distrust of language reminds us of Beckett who might have been an important influence on her. But Murdoch is faced with the serious problem of the value of art as such, because, as a moral philosopher, she is concerned with truth and goodness. Debates about the value and danger of art naturally leads her back to the Western source of the debate, Plato. In her book, *The Fire and the Sun : Why Plato Banished the Artists*, she vigorously explicates Plato's views on the subject, his objections to art, but finally awards a victory to art. Plato originated a metaphysical theory about the nature of mimesis. For him, art is far removed from the truth, springs from merely vicarious knowledge, is the product of the inferior part of the soul, and is harmful, because it nourishes those passions which should be educated and disciplined.

Murdoch adds to this her own objections to art. There is something magical in the nature of art. It is an attempt to achieve omnipotence through personal fantasy and is the abode of wish-fulfilment power-mania, and illusory unities. But, at the same time, Murdoch looks upon great art as something lofty, something that is able to explain religion to mankind. It is not possible to capture reality, and thus, all art lies. But good art according to Murdoch lies its way into the truth. Moreover, since no art is perfect, all art partakes of a certain degree of moral ambiguity.

.Along with three books on philosophy Murdoch has written numerous philosophical treatises, and it is impossible to discuss here her philosophy in detail. But I have tried to offer an elementary explication of her basic philosophical thought because her philosophy is closely related to her fiction. In her book, *Sartre : Romantic Rationalist* she accepts Sartre the philosopher and Sartre the novelist as one, and thus reveals her own interest in using the novel as a way of developing philosophical ideas. Her criticism of Sartre makes clear her own artistic intentions. She says that Sartre makes a serious mistake—he wants to set the world to order and to reduce it to the intelligible through art. In her most celebrated essay, "Against Dryness" Murdoch says that instead of this,

> "what we require is a renewed sense of the difficulty and complexity of moral life and the opacity of persons."

And in her essay "The Sublime and the Beautiful Revisited" she argued that :

> "Contingency must be defended, for it is the essence of

> personality.... A novel must be a house fit for free characters to live in; and to combine form with respect for reality with all its contingent ways is the highest art of prose."

But she has been plagued by an uncertainty about her success in achieving this ideal. As she told Frank Kermode, she has tried

> "to create a lot of people who are not me. ...yet often it turns out in the end that something about the structure of the work itself, the myth as it were of the work, has drawn all these people into a sort of spiral, or into a kind of form which ultimately is the form of one's own mind."[18]

Grappling with problems facing an artist with a philosopher's precise mind, Murdoch in "Against Dryness" divided the twentieth century novel into two types, the crystalline or journalistic,

> "that is, either a small quasi-allegorical object portraying the human condition and not containing 'characters' in the nineteenth century sense, or else it is a large shapeless quasi-documentary object, the degenerate descendant of the nineteenth century novel, telling, with pale conventional characters, some straightforward story enlivened with empirical facts."[19]

None of these types, argues Murdoch, solves the problems about human personality. Instead,

> "The modern writer...attempts to console us with myths or stories."[20]

I think we have now come to the most difficult part of our discussion. Iris Murdoch is a prolofic writer and has written twenty-three novels. A serious thinker and artist, she shows continuous development. She employs various techniques in various novels and I think that it is impossible to do justice to her as a novelist in the course of a single paper. While her first novel *Under the Net* is written in the picaresque mode, her interest in intricate plots becomes apparent in the next four novels. *The Flight from an Enchanter* develops an elaborate and fantastic plot which verges on the supernatural. Whereas in *The Sandcastle* the emphasis falls on the realistic background, in *The Bell*, one of the most artistically coherent of her novels, the symbolic background is fully developed, and used to enhance our understanding of the characters who exist in their own right and never become overtly subjugated to the needs of the plot. In *The Unicorn* and *The Red and the Green* the scene shifts from London and the Counties to Ireland and while the first, a historical novel, deals with moral problems of a young Anglo-Irish soldier whose loyalties are divided during the Easter Rising,

The Unicorn repeats the religious symbolism of *The Bell*. In *The Unicorn* and *The Time of the Angels* she explores the gothic romance at the expense of her aspirations of marrying realism and fantasy.

Murdoch has repeatedly spoken of the need for realism which often meant avoiding designing, patterning, symbol and myth. But in practice she seems to write in a technique that she most disapproves of. As she matures as a writer she becomes more and more involved in the intricacies of the plot and though subtleties of the human mind and the details of life engage her, we do feel that her tightly wound plots relentlessly impose a pattern on the characters she creates. Yet, even this is not the last word about her novelistic technique, because in the eighties she seems to take a turn in another direction. The problem that faces any person trying to introduce Murdoch's novelistic world is that she keeps on renewing herself, keeps on changing and growing. In three late novels *Postscript*, *The Good Apprentice*, and *The Book and the Brotherhood* she seems to abandon the closely structured balanced plots for more carelessly constructed sprawling novels in which form is obscured by too much adherence to contingency. She concentrates on the act of describing, and these recent novels have become formally unweildly, lacking in the strong shapeliness for which Murdoch has expressed admiration. *The Good Apprentice* is a novel in three sections, and in the central and longest section of the book "Seegard" Murdoch leaves her realistic technique behind and moves into the world of pure fantasy. "Seegard" is the name of the huge mist-girt architectural folly erected by Jesse Baltram by the sea, a beautiful, uncanny creation, half-real, belonging to the world of art and magic, a city state whose habits and manners are superbly evoked for us. We find here a sudden and shocking transition out of a believable contemporary London into the Seegard world.

In order to understand the world of Murdoch's novels we have to understand her overriding preoccupations : the theme of power, of the inability of language to express reality, the theme of responsibility and freedom, and the meaning of love. Often all these themes are fused together in the apparently contradictory concept of responsibility as an essential part of liberty. These are the themes that shape her novels and I would like to put emphasis on a limited number of novels to understand these. This, I think, will enable us to understand her better, and to avoid broad generalisations.

In his *Modes of Modern Writing* David Lodge focuses on two types of writing : realistic and modernist. Realistic writing, he says, emphasizes the uniqueness of things, persons, places, where modernist writing aspires to a concentrated symbolic formal unity. He suggests that a possible programme for a new writing might reside in the conscious attempt to combine these two modes.[21] Murdoch's avowed aim in the novel approaches this project. In an interview in 1958, after publishing her first four novels she made a distinction between the open and the closed novel which I think should be quoted in full :

> "I find myself thinking in terms of two kinds of novels which might be called "open" and "closed", and I cannot at the moment decide which kind I want to write : perhaps, more or less alternately both. The open novel contains a lot of characters who rush about independently, each one eccentric and self-centered, the plot to some extent situates them in a pattern but does not integrate them into a single system. The closed novel has fewer characters and tends to draw them as it were, toward a single point. *Under the Net* and *The Flight from an Enchanter* were, I think, 'closed', *The Sandcastle* and *The Bell* 'open'. The advantage of the open novel is that it is bright and airy and the characters move about freely; it is more like life as it is normally lived. Its disadvantage is that it may become loose in texture and it is more difficult to make the structure evident. A closed novel is more closely integrated but may be more claustrophobic in atmosphere and the characters may lose their sense of freedom. Ideally, and if one were a great writer, one could, I think, combine both of these things in a single work and not have to oscillate between them."[22]

Apparently the interviewer made a mistake and the terms 'open' and 'closed' were reversed because the first two fall in the category of 'open' novels and the second two are really 'closed' according to her definition. But her aim becomes clear from this interview.

Her first novel *Under the Net,* we have seen, was published at a time when the neo-naturalistic novels of the Angry Young Men were attracting attention, and was hailed as a Movement novel. It won immediate acclaim for its wit, humour, realistic description, and intelligence. Even this first novel opened up an astonishingly varied world. Her powers of minute observation and detailed comedy connects this novel to contemporary film techniques, and yet the acute human observations and the philosophical questioning already suggests her late development both as a symbolic novelist and a psychological novelist with an uncanny power to illuminate the motives that lie beneath the surface of human behaviour.

The first-person male narrator, Jake Douaghue like Murdoch, is an Irishman brought up in London. At the opening of the novel he comes back from France and his squire Finn tells him that Madge, who had allowed them to live rent-free in her apartment was getting married, and that he was now homeless. Now starts a long chain of journeys with mistakes about who loves whom. These journeys represent a mixture of flight and quest. The hero is an impressionable, impulsive, restless romantic, and the novel is mainly concerned with his rootlessness and quest for stability. The novel ends with Jake coming back to London with a menial job, having refused an offer of a fortune in the film industry.

What distinguishes this novel from contemporary novels by the Movement writers and also nineteenth century picaresque novels, is the philosophical underpinning. Jake is a recognizable type, the typical jaunty anti-hero of his time. But it is his relationship with Hugo that is the central theme of the novel. Actually Hugo is the other hero of the novel—a truer and less visible kind of anti-hero. Jake is the existentialist hero who tries to assert or find himself whereas Hugo is the mystical hero trying to discipline and diminish himself. The central theme of the novel is Jake's fascination with Hugo, the misunderstandings between them and their peculiar relationship. Actually the time Jake spends with Hugo allows him to see the truth. Jake early notes that to try to place him, as he first attempted, was a failure of taste, which showed a peculiar insensitivity to his unique intellectual and moral quality.[23]

Hugo is suspicious, like Beckett, of the ability of language to represent the real. This suspicion is actually life-giving because it is born of a love of truth and a love of the real. Jake starts seeing truth and reality through his conversations with Hugo :

> "For Hugo each thing was astonishing, delightful, complicated, and mysterious. During these conversations I began to see the world anew."[24]

Hugo's impact on Jake is philosophical, but he is against general theories. He rather wants to know the nature of each thing. He speaks of the inadequacy of language in representing reality, and concludes that

> "The whole language is a machine for making falsehoods."[25]

He tells Jake,

> "Try describing anything, our conversation for instance, and see how absolutely instinctively you....

> 'Touch it up?'
>
> 'It's deeper than that, said Hugo. The language just won't let you present it as it really is."[26]

Jake, trying to put down his discussions with Hugo writes in his book *The Silencer* :

> "What I speak of is the real decision as we experience it; and here the movement away from theory and generality is the movement towards truth. All theorizing is flight. We must be ruled by the situation itself and this is unutterably particular. Indeed it is something to which we can never get close enough, however hard we may try as it were to crawl under the net."[27]

This takes us back to Murdoch's plea that art should concern itself with contingency. As Bradbury sees it,

> "Hugo, like his author, argues too that art works against theory, but presses the logic towards silence. This leaves Jake with the problem of picking his way between the extremes of theory and silence, the unutterable particularity of human experience and their social mediation as art."[28]

The presence of Lefty Todd offers another point of departure for the artist and makes the dilemma for Jake more serious. He is the dialectical opposite of Hugo, and argues for a practical and political unity of theory and practice. He offers a different role for the artist and intellectual and urges Jake into political responses. By refusing an offer of an easy script-writing job Jake commits himself to the solitary exploration of his intellectual role amid these options. The job he takes as an orderly in a hospital is an alternative choice that unites the aesthetic with the social :

> ["It occurred to me that to spend half the day doing manual work might be very calming to the nerves of one who was spending the other half doing intellectual work and I could not imagine why I had not thought before of this way of living, which could ensure that no day could pass without something having been done, and so keep that sense of uselessness, which grows in prolonged periods of sterility, away from me forever."[29]]

Jake's brief encounter with Hugo at the hospital helps him to remove the misunderstandings about people, and the end is a moral celebration : a recognition of the individuality of persons and of things as they are. The novel ends with Jake's education complete. He has balanced the demands of intellectual and practical life, and he has renewed his creative energy.

The Flight from an Enchanter remains important because of its central theme : power. Its central figure, an enchanter, Mischa Fox is obsessed with the desire for power, and tries to control the lives of everybody around him in various ways. The plot is elaborate and verges on the supernatural, and this starts a chain of later novels that connect the world of her novels with the fantastic scenarios we meet in the novels of William Golding or Muriel Spark. But what is more important is that this enchanter figure with his craze for power growing in intensity in the later novels, becomes a leitmotif in many of her novels, and is central to the schematization that affects her later work. In *The Red and the Green* Millie Kinnward as a charismatic agent draws the other characters through a field of force. One Andrew, loses his virginity to Millie; another, Pat Dumay, hard and violent, wants her for sexual satisfaction. Christopher, her betrothed, wants to see her, and the elderly withdrawn figure of Barney comes to spy on her out of a kind of love. In *A Severed Head* a comic realism concerned with social relationships passes on to an account of love as morally imperative by virtue of its totemism, its violence, its irrationality. Martin Lynch-Gibbon enters a world of control and power and has to drop his talent for a gentler world. The enchanter figure is the psychoanalyst Palmer Anderson. Martin's wife Antonia wants to leave him for Palmer, and Palmer, identified at one point with Dionysus, argues for a relaxation of social and moral rules. He wants to include Martin in a sort of ménage-a-trois and suggests like a Dostoievsky villain that "All is permitted." With his anthropologist half-sister Honer Klein, he is a modern day magician, expert in the workings of the human mind, and in understanding the forces that underlie ordinary 'civilized' conduct.

This theme of the psychological manipulation of characters through some devilish power-crazy maniac gets a comic treatment that ultimately turns to tragedy in *A Fairly Honourable Defeat.* Julius, the lover of Morgan, bets her ten guineas that he will be able to break off the homosexual relationship between Axel and Simon. By subtle and devilish suggestions and careful manipulations he succeeds in engineering a love-affair between Morgan and her brother-in-law, the impractical philosopher Rupert. Julius reminds us of Iago and Iachimo, and what is contested is a harshly cynical and sour view of the inconstancy of the human heart.

Julius' devilry is placed in direct opposition to the fascinating saintliness of Tallis, Morgan's husband. Although his diabolical opposite finds him a "strange little person" he acts decisively at key moments like the time he strikes at the hoodlums in the restaurant. Tallis is the only "good" man in Murdoch's novels who occupies a central position. One important Platonic axiom expressed in Murdoch's fiction is that the mind in its relentless egoism habitually mistakes false images of the good (eidola) for good itself, so that even the most spiritually advanced human beings, the aspiring saints, cannot escape the dense net of illusion created by personal desire. She remarked in an interview that no one in her books, except Tallis gets very far in discarding selfishness.[30] She herself characterizes this novel as a "a theological myth", a "theological allegory", "a religious allegory".[31] Tallis is a symbolic character. It is his job, as it were, to be good. You end to think that a good character is not strong, but Tallis is strong.[32] Tallis appears as a genuine Christ figure, emblematic of redemptive suffering. But the Christian myth of the dying God-man is not so important for Murdoch. As her opposition between the devilish Julian and the other power-crazy people and Tallis imply, renunciation for her is always of the 'self', never of the body only. She seeks not meek powerlessness but non-power, the absence of a dangerous charisma or psychological power over others. In her more recent novel, *The Good Apprentice*, Stuart appears as just such a Christ figure. His is the same passivity that arouses more self-defensive hatred than love and he has been compared to Prince Myshkin in *The Idiot*. Jesse Baltram, the tyrant who has created Seegard, cannot stand him, and in their encounter where he expresses his hatred we find the clearest, purest confrontation in Murdoch's world of the egoist and the saint.

Because of her faith in contingency, in the arbitrary and the unexpected in life, Murdoch's novels are full of violent incidents which are often used to purge away the typical network of characters who are grouped around a charismatic figure. Floods (*Bruno's Dream*), fire (*The Italian Girl*), fatal car accidents (*An Accidental Man, A World Child*), murder (*The Black Prince*) and *The Sacred and Profane Love Machine*) drownings (*A Fairly Honourable Defeat*), international terrorism (*The Sacred and Profane Love Machine*) and suicides abound in her novels, and she has even been described as a modern descendant of Mrs. Radcliffe for her taste for the violent and the strange. Often, as in *A Fairly Honourable Defeat,* violent death is used as an easy solution to the human problems, and the death of Hildoc's husband Rupert takes the characters out of an impossible situation.

But this criticism overlooks one of Murdoch's important preoccupations. Death and violence are important in her novels in a deeper sense. In *Bruno's Dream* her most Beckettian novel, reminding us of *Malone Dies*, the long dying of Bruno provides a kind of constant point of spiritual reference. In *The Nice and the Good* a serious brush with death generates a central figure's (Eugene, who is a person displaced by war, and lives, appropriately, in an air-raid shelter) renunciation and, reorientation. The violent accident in which Anne, Hilary Burde's mistress and the wife of his friend, dies, casts a shadow on the whole of his life in *A Word Child*. The important point here is that Murdoch wants to replace the Freudian idea of psychological necessity—of emotional compulsion—with a necessity inherent in the cosmos. She replaces freedom of choice with the equally transcendent idea of accident or chance. She makes a distinction not between determinism and freedom, but between mechanism on the one hand, and the linked forces of Necessity and Chance on the other. By mechanism she understands psychological or material causality as opposed to a truly moral causality that includes both Necessity and Chance. In "The Sovereignty of the Good" Murdoch explains that so-called freedom of choice or freedom of will applies to only a small area of our mental activity. The suggestion is that in the process of so-called choice, "the forces which are dark to me have already made the decision".[33]

As Hilary Burde says about the accident that has darkened his life :

> "Yet such things happen to men, lives are thus ruined thus tainted and darkened and irrevocably spoilt, wrong turnings are taken and persisted in and those who make one mistake wreck all the rest out of frenzy, even out of pique."[34]

In a recent book Harold Bloom praises her Shakespearean facility for intricate double plots, and ranks her below only Freud and Proust as a provocative theorist of love. After a temporary dip in her reputation in the 1960's Murdoch is again being recognised as a serious novelist who entertains with her brilliantly contrived plots, and, at the same time celebrates the wonder and unpredictability of the very real characters who people her world. Her dark world has been compared to the world of Dostoevski's novels, and we hope this extraordinary novelist will attract increasing critical attention.

NOTES AND REFERENCES

1. Henry James, "The Future of the Novel" (1899) reprinted in Henry James, *The Future of the Novel* (New York : Vintage, 1956) edited by Leon Edel.
2. Malcolm Bradbury, *Possibilities : Essays on the State of the Novel*, London 1973.

3. A. Alvarez. Quoted in Blake Morrison, *The Movement : English Poetry and Fiction of the 1950's*, London, 1980.
4. Quoted from and Oxford Magazine by David Marquand in "Lucky Jim and the Labour Party", "Universities and Left Review", I. (Spring, 1957), 57.
5. Malcolm Bradbury, "The Novel" in C.B. Cox, A.E. Dyson edited *The Twentieth Century Mind,* London, 1972, p. 342.
6. Iris Murdoch, *Under the Net*, Penguin Books, 1977, p. 106.
7. *Ibid*., p. 72.
8. "Recontres avee Iris Murdoch", Jean-Louis Chevalier (ed.) Université de Caen, France.
9. "John Haffenden Talks to Iris Murdoch", Literary Review, LVIII, April 31—5.
10. The respect felt by the 1930's generation for a broad or cosmopolitan culture was a thing of the past. Dixon in *Lucky Jim* finds the cultural atmosphere at the Welches especially unbearable because there is a reading of Anouilh. —"Why couldn't they have Chosen an English Play?" Actually the imposition of a £ 50 travel allowance discouraged foreign travel, and the British intellectuals made of virtue of necessity.
11. Conradi, Peter J., *Iris Murdoch, The Saint and the Artist,* Macmillan, 1986.
12. Albert Camus at an interview. Quoted in Chatterjee, Margaret, *The Existentialist Outlook*, Delhi, 1973, p. 6.
13. Bigsby, in Ziegler, H. and Bigsby C.W.E. (eds.), *The Radical Imagination and the Liberal Tradition : Interviews with English and American Novelists,* London, 1982, pp. 209-30.
14. Conradi, Peter J., *Iris Murdoch, The Saint and the Artist,* Macmillan, 1986.
15. "The Sublime and the Beautiful Revisited", Yale Review, XLIX 1959, pp. 269-70.
16. 'On "God" and "Good" ' in Murdoch, Iris, *The Sovereignty of the Good*, London, 1970.
17. Iris Murdoch, *Sartre : Romantic Rationalist,* London, 1953, ch. X.
18. Interview in "Partisan Review", Spring, 1963.
19. Iris Murdoch, "Against Dryness", printed in Malcolm Bradbury ed. *The Novel Today,* Glasgow, 1977, p. 27.
20. *Ibid*., p. 28.
21. D. Lodge *The Modes of Modern Writing : Metaphor, Metonymy and the Typology of Modern Literature*, London, 1977.
22. Anon., *Mainly About Authors*, Bookman, Nov. 1958, p. 26.
23. *Under the Net,* Penguin Books, 1974, p. 58.
24. *Ibid*., p. 58.
25. Iris Murdoch, *Under the Net*, Penguin, 1974, p. 60.
26. *Ibid*., p. 59.
27. *Ibid*., pp. 80-81.
28. Malcolm Bradbury, *Possibilities*, p. 243.
29. *Under the Net,* p. 209.
30. Bigsby 1982, in Ziegler H. and Bigsby, C.W.E. (eds.) "The Radical Imagination and the Liberal Tradition : Interviews with English and American Novelists", (London), p. 220.

31. Bellany, "An Interview" p. 135.
    Caen, "An Interview", p. 75.
    Bigsby, "An Interview", p. 229.
32. John Haffenden, "John Haffendem talks to Iris Murdoch", Literary Review, 58 (1983), 34.
33. Iris Murdoch, *The Sovereignty of the Good,* London, 1970, p. 36.
34. *A Word Child*, London, 1975, p. 221.

4

Mark Twain and Post-modernism—*A Connecticut Yankee* as Historiographic Metafiction

DR. A.H. TAK
Department of English
University of Kashmir, Srinagar

In any traditional history of postmodernism, Mark Twain seems to play no role at all. Like some other nineteenth-century Anglo-American novelists—Hawthorne, Melville, Thackeray, Trollope, George Eliot or Hardy—he is regarded as having nothing positive to contribute to the coming of postmodernism, more surprising, he is not even employed in any extended way as contrast or foil, against which the new dispensation may be measured. He is simply omitted without a word of explanation—which implies that his works look forward to few of the ideas and social conditions of the present. Moreover, it suggests that Mark Twain has very little to contribute to future reconceptualization of our discipline, including the interdisciplinary projects so characteristic of postmodernism. The present paper, therefore, is a digression from the main trend of Mark Twain scholarship because here an attempt has been made to analyse *A Connecticut Yankee In King Arthur's Court* in the light of the postmodernist concept of 'historiographic metafiction' given by Linda Hutcheon in *A Poetics of Postmodernism : History, Theory, Fiction*. Identifying the postmodern elements in Mark Twain, it is presumed, will not only help us to re-evaluate our portrait of the novelist but will also make us recognise that postmodernism is not dawning of a new age but the realization of certain possibilities within western society that were salient even in the time of Twain.

The term 'postmodernism', as agreed by its advocates and detractors alike, has no stable meaning and refers to so many different things for so many different people that the 'multiplicity of references' has itself been theorized as a major lesson of postmodernism : "that terms are by no means guaranteed their meanings, and that these meanings can be appropriated and redefined for different purposes, different contexts, and, more important, different causes".[1] What the postmodern writings of both history and literature have taught us is that both history and fiction are discourses, that both constitute systems of signification by which we make sense of the past. It can be asserted that postmodern effects two simultaneous moves : it reinstalls historical contexts as significant and even determining, but in so doing it problematizes the entire notion of historical knowledge. This problematizing has been in the foreground of much contemporary literary theory, fiction, and philosophy of history from Hayden White to Paul Veyne. When Hayden White calls history "a true novel" he is not only signalling the two genre's shared conventions like selection, organization, dieresis and employment but also challenging the implied assumptions of historical statements : objectivity, neutrality, impersonality and transparency of representation.[2] Even E.L. Doctorow's notion that "history is a kind of fiction in which we live and hope to survive and fiction is a kind of speculative history"[3] points towards the same direction. The metafictionality of novels acknowledging their own construction, selection and order, but shown to be historically determined acts is what is called "historiographic metafiction".[4] This phrase is used to refer to those well known and popular novels like *The Public Burning, The Book of Daniel, Ragtime, The Armies of The Night, Lincoln : A Novel, Midnight's Children* etc. Which are both intensely self-reflexive and yet paradoxically lay claim to historical events and personages. Historiographic metafiction refutes the commonsense methods of distinguishing between historical fact and fiction. It refutes the view that only history has a truth claim, both by questioning the ground of that claim in historiography and by asserting that both history and fiction are discourses, human constructs, signifying systems, and both derive their major claim to truth from that identity. In other words, the meaning and shape are not in the events, but in the systems which make the past events into present historical "facts".

This perspective will redefine and clarify, if not resolve the vexing problem, which Susan Harris and a dozen of other critics have tried to discuss : the status of *A Connecticut Yankee in King Authur's Court* as a historical novel. According to Harris the novel's presenting the historical reality of King Arthur's Court is a sham and according to James D. Williams, "Mark Twain's attempts to historical accuracy in *A Connecticut Yankee* were sporadic and strictly limited by the demands of farce, outrage, or the theme of progress".[5] Even the critics like Lorch, Baetzholds, Soloman, Smith and the earlier reviewers like William Thomas Stead point out that the novel contains "much strange misreading of history" and Mark Twain's attempt at historical accuracy were conditioned by various other social aims and he borrowed from a vast number of sources in order to accomplish his task.[6] The general consensus is that Mark Twain "made no serious efforts to present accurately the life of the day" but "forced history to serve his own views," and looked for "historical examples of cruelty and injustice as the cores for successive narrative episodes."[7] Similarly the critics who have concentrated on the social criticism contained in the book can be divided in two groups : those who recognise Twain's overall condemnation of multifarious aspects of human lot including Arthurian milieu and all it suggests; and those who have seen Hank Morgan as an ambivalent protagonist symbolizing mechanistic progress and democratic ideals but, at the same time, regrets the loss of inherent in a past romantic age.[8]

Some of these misconceptions about the book, *A Connecticut Yankee in King Arthur's Court* grew out of the fact that it is not a conventional historical novel like Thackeray's *Henry Esmond* or Dickens's *A Tale of Two Cities* where history has been used as a means to an end. It is on the other hand, a combination of novel, romance and history and Mark Twain's deliberate attempt to rescue himself from self-destructive mockery by 'grabbing onto a historical moment' and as a means of strengthening the truth and force of his fictional apprehension of life by extending it into a further range of actual experience. It may be pointed out here that Mark Twain's combining of novel, romance, and history in a parodic way, as will be analysed later, itself affiliates *A Connecticut Yankee* with Doctorow's *Ragtime*. Coover's *The Public Burning*, Rushdie's *Midnight's Children* and similar other postmodern novels in which the distinction between traditional genres is blurred. That Mark Twain himself was conscious of such a bold adventure, particularly in the nineteenth-century, can be testified by the fact that he wrote Howells shortly before the book was published : "I don't think I'll send out any other press copy—except perhaps to Stedman. I'm not writing for those parties who miscall themselves critics and I don't care to have them paw the book at all."[9] Again, it is absolutely wrong to presume that

Mark Twain was not interested in writing history. A proper evaluation of the novel and the background material in the form of note-book entries and letters would indicate that one of the main aims of Mark Twain was to write a history. It can be noticed from his claim (in early 1886) that he had been "saturating" himself with "the atmosphere of the day and the subject" and from a letter (he wrote on 16 November) to Mrs. Fairbanks that he was "after the life of that day, that is all; to picture it; to try to get into it; to see how it feels and seems."[10] Even after twenty years of the publication of the novel, he spoke of having attempted in *A Connecticut Yankee* to imagine and set forth "not just the English life of Arthur's day but ... the whole of the Middle Ages."[11] Williams, very rightly, points out : "Aside from *Le Morte D' Arthur* itself, and perhaps and handful of chronicles in the Bohn Library, Mark Twain relied on secondary sources for his knowledge of Medieval life."[12] Williams indicates a number of chronicles and historical works like Lecky's *History of European Morals.* and *History of England in the Eighteenth Century*; Henri Forneron's *The Court of Charles II, 1639-1734*; George Standring's *People's History of English Aristocracy*; Charles Bell's *Slavery in the United States*; and a dozen other works which, according to him, Mark Twain used in the book, concluding, thereby, that even Mark Twain "forced history to serve his own views."[13] Williams wrote in 60s without taking into consideration postmodernism's claims that "the only 'genuine historicity' becomes that which would openly acknowledge its own discussive, contingent identity".[14] At present we know that novels like *The Public Burning* and *Legs* assert that the past did exist prior to its "inter textualization" into either fiction or history. They also show that both genres unavoidably construct as they textualize that past. The "real" referent of their language once existed; but it is only accessible to us today in textualized form, documents, eye-witness accounts, archives etc.

In the novel *A Connecticut Yankee in King Arthur's Court*, therefore, Mark Twain demonstrates his historical knowledge as well as his ability to render historical reality in fiction. In the first sentence of the 'Preface' he states "The ungentle laws and customs touched upon in this tale are historical, and the episodes which are used to illustrate them are also historical".[15] However, he adds "It is not pretended that these laws and customs existed in England in the sixth century." These statements sound confusing and critics have attempted to solve the confusion by relating them to source materials without producing any fruitful results and adding hardly anything substantial to the understanding of the novel. Some critics like Henry Nash Smith assert that the novel is a historical allegory whereas others like Hoffman call it an allegorical history in the sense that "the historical quality of King Arthur's realm is presented allegorically rather than realistically." Hoffman proceeds to compare the Historians' rendering of facts like Industrial America, rise of Roman Catholic Church, problem of slavery in Old South, and American Imperialism with Mark Twain's rendering of them in the novel, the main focus, however, being on source hunting.

Any evaluation or analysis of *A Connecticut Yankee* should begin with Hank Morgan, the narrator and Mark Twain's attitude toward him. Mark Twain portrayed him as a character with "rude animal side," "his circus side" but at the same time a man with "the god heart" and "the high intent".[16] In the book he introduces him as "the curious stranger" with "marvelous familiarity with ancient armor" drifting away "imperceptibly out of this world and time, and into some remote era and old forgotten country."[17] Not only this, according to Twain "Exactly as I would speak of my nearest personal friends or enemies, or my most familiar neighbours, he spoke of Sir Bedivere, Sir Bors de Ganis, Sir Lancelot of the Lake, Sir Galahad, and all other great names of the Table Round" (11). At the end of "A word of Explanation" we are told how Hank Morgan gave Twain a manuscript which he had prepared; "First, I kept a journal; then by and by, after years, I took the journal and turned in into a book. How long ago that was!" (16). Even in chapter XLIV "A Postscript by Clarence", after everything is destroyed and Hank is send to sleep by Merlin for thirteen centuries, we are told : "It is agreed that if any one of us ever escapes alive from this place, he will write the fact here, and loyally hide this Manuscript with the Boss, our dear good Chief, whose property it is, be he alive or dead" (318).

Hank Morgan, The Boss and the narrator of *A Connecticut Yankee* is projected by Mark Twain as a historian and the writer of the surviving "Manuscript". All the Characters, illusions, references are seen through him and form part of his manuscript. Hank Morgan; "a Yankee of the Yankees—and practical...nearly barren of sentiment...or poetry" (14), has not only lived the history he is describing but also suffered it. He is not only familiar with machine shops, news offices, train-butchers, oil fields and steam boats etc. but such events of terror and pathos as the "old weary tale" of the woman dying of small pox, (Ch. XXIX), or the retaliatory hangings by the Mob after a baron has been murdered and his house burned down (Ch. XXX). He not only describes social, political, economic and religious conditions of the sixth century but also analysis minutely such events and customs of the century as the belief in Witchcraft (256), the slave trade (Ch. XXXIV), the organization of tournaments (Ch. IX) and even the matrimonial conventions (117 - 19). While talking of the nation as a whole Hank writes that most of king Arthur's British nation were slaves : "The truth was, the nation as a body was in the world for one object and one only : to grovel before king and Church and nobel, to slave for them, sweat blood for them, starve that they might be fed, work that they might play, drink misery to the dregs that they might be happy, go naked that they might wear silks and Jewels, pay taxes that they might be spared for paying them,..." (54). He criticizes the ideals like "the divine right of kings" and "supremacy of Church" which "introduced heritable ranks and aristocracies, and taught all the Christian populations of the earth to bow down to them and worship them". (56). At the sametime, he points out : "I will say this much for the nobility : that, tyrannical, murderous, repacious and morally rotten as they were, they were deeply and enthusiastically religious". (104). In Chapter XXIII, he gives a lucid description of the hermits whereas in chapter XXXIII "Sixth-Century Political Economy" he analysis the basis of the economic structure of the country saying "that 'high wages' and 'low wages' are phrases that do not mean anything in the world until you find out which of them will by the most" (236). Hank Morgan elucidates the political system as well, saying that "some of those laws were too bad, altogether too bad. A master might kill his slave for nothing : for more spite, malice, or to pass time.... A gentleman could kill a free commoner, and pay for him—cash or garden truck. A noble could kill a noble without expense.... Anybody could kill somebody, except the commoner and slave; these had no privileges" (115). One of the most painful illustrations of there "unequal laws unto a savage race"[18] is given in Chapter XXXV "A Pitiful Incident" (257-59) in which a van is described in which there was "a cart with a coffin in it, and on the coffin sat a comely young girl of about eighteen suckling a baby, which she squeezed to her brest..." (256). This young girl was a happy married woman whose husband was send to sea where he died and now she was being punished for stealing "a piece of linen cloth of the value of a fourth part of a cent, thinking to sell it and save her child" (257). Hank Morgan terms it as "a sample of one sort of London society", "A law sends this poor young thing to death—and it is right. But another law had placed her where she must commit her crime or starve, with her child—and before god that law is responsible for both her crime and her ignominious death!" (*Ibid*).

Our historian becomes an unreliable narrator only when he abandons himself to his dreams. According to Berkove, "The perceptive reader, therefore, can no longer look to Hank for a satisfactory account of objective reality but must seek it through interpretation, by paying closer attention to Twain's strategies".[19] Starting from a very vital premise that "the novel's abundant references to dreams are purposeful and crucial parts of both its structure and its themes", Berkove concludes his seven page study just by saying that the novel "is not really about Hank, or sixth century England, or nineteenth century America either, for that matter".[20] I think the novel is about all these things and the best way to understand it is to analyse in some detail the reference to dreams. The first reference to "dream" occurs in Chapter V, 'An Inspiration; when Hank Morgan awakens in the dungeon of Camelot and thinks "well, what an astonishing dream I've had' immediately, with the reappearance of Clarence, he resigns himself : "All right.... Let the dream go on; I'm in no hurry". Clarence brings news that Hank will be burned on the next day and "evokes a reaction from Hank which unexpectedly discloses an essential similarity between "dream" and "reality", and illuminates how arbitrary and unimportant the distinction between the two states may be".[21] Hank's own statements testify this argument : "I was fast getting adjusted to my situation and circumstances. For a time, I used to wake up, mornings, and smile at my "dream"... and at last I was fully able to realize that I was actually living in the sixth century, and in Arthur's Court, not a lunatic asylum" (52). Even in "Final P.S. by M.T." Mark Twain indicates that after he went to Hank's room "his mutterings and ejaculations went on" (319). In his mutterings and prior to his death Hank makes reference to so many things including "dreams". "And such dreams! Such strange and awful dreams, Sandy! Dreams that were as real as reality—delirium, of course but so real!" (320). Hank breaths his last muttering"...death is nothing, let it come, but not with those dreams, not with the torture of those hideous dreams—I cannot endure that again" (320). The important point to note in these remarks is Hank's confusing dream and reality : as he speaks, it is clear that his Arthurian dream is now reality to him and that his return to the nineteenth century "with an abyss of thirteen centuries yawning...between me and all that is dear to me"(320) is not a simple dream but something more complex which needs to be solved.

In order to understand the basis of this complexity it should be kept in mind that the novel develops on two distinct plot lines and themes : that man's history is determined by the scope of his "dreams" of what can be labelled as imagination; that history is determined by the 'cause-and-effect' relationship between events over which man has no control. Mark Twain's reference to "transmigration of souls" and "transposition of epoches" (11), followed by Hank Morgan's narrative in which he mentions how a fellow called Hercules "laid me out with a crusher alongside the head that made everything crack" till "I came to again" (15) and met the knight who led him to king Arthur's Court clearly indicate that history, as conceived by Mark Twain, is a state of mind, a kind of potential narrative where the events of the past exist independent of the connections we forge between them by the power of imagination. Following this argument it can be asserted that the novel, *A Connecticut Yankee*, blurs the distinction not only between "dream" and "reality" but also between history and fiction by proposing a dream-like past as a stand-in for a nightmare present, and thereby achieves a clearer vision of the time than even modern historians have not been able to piece together. At the best Twain has shown, there are many and subtle ways to respect both the documentable and the imaginative without sacrificing either to other. The artist has no monopoly on imagination, the historian no monopoly on the past. The writer of either history or fiction has to be discriminating, synthesizing and advocative. Neither can afford to ignore the other, especially the other in himself—this is what relates him to the postmodern historiographic metafiction writers and theoreticians like Hayden White, Dominick La Capra, E.L. Doctorow, Robert Coover, Norman Mailer and others.

There is, however, another way of looking at the whole issue. In *A Connecticut Yankee* Hank Morgan, the historian, presents himself ultimately not as metaphorical witness or imaginary participant of the sixth century but as a scholar who explicitly participated in the events. In his manuscript there is not only a vivid evocation of a particular period, with due representation from all classes involved, but also the description of historical personages. By making it appear "strange" or fictional Mark Twain brings home the fact that using a novel to understand history necessarily produces as many difficulties as using history to understand a novel, looking at a piece of fiction as a sort of expression of the age in which it is written. In either case, we are hampered by distance between our time and the author's as well as between the author and his own time. The only historical position we take, like the author we are reading, is our own because we were neither with the author when he wrote, nor in the period of which he wrote. In other words, central to *A Connecticut Yankee* is the "concern for the way we know history" that Avrom Fleischman sees as characteristic of all serious historical novels.[22] By creating a fictional world that mediates English history and literature, Mark Twain suggests that history is fictional; much of our literature promotes illusions about history, and literature can never be independent of the historical world—all these being the major concerns of postmodernism.

NOTES

1. Andrew Ross, "Introduction" in *Universial Abandon? The Politics of Postmodernism*, ed. Ross (Minneapolis, 1988), XI.
2. Hayden White, *Metahistory* (Baltimore, 1973), 3; see also his "The Historical text as literary Artifact", *Clio* 3 : 3 (1974), 299.
3. See, Doctorow's lecture and interview published in Richard Trenner ed. *Essays and Conversations,* (Princerton, NJ, 1983), particularly pp. 39, 52.
4. Linda Hutcheon, *A Poetics of Postmodernism : History, Theory and Fiction* (New York, 1988). Most of my arguments on 'historiographic metafiction' are based on this book, particularly on the Chapter of the title.
5. Susan K. Harris, *Mark Twain's Escape from Time* (Columbia, 1982), 58; James D. Williams, "The use of History in Mark Twain's *A Connecticut Yankee", PMLA* 80 (1965), 102.
6. See *The Literary World* (Boston) XXI (15 Feb. 1890) 52-53; *The Review of Reviews* (Feb. 1890), 144. Also, Fred w. Lorch, "Hawaian Feudalism and Mark Twain's *A Connecticut Yankee in King Arthur's Court", American Scholar,* XXX (March 1958), 55; Howad G. Baetzhold, "The course of Composition of *A Connecticut Yankee* : A Reinterpretation", *American* Literature, XXXIII (May 1961), 210; Roger B. Solomon, *Twain and The Image of History* (Yale Studies in English, No. 150; New Haven, 1961), 102; Hanry Nash Smith, *Mark Twain* (Cambridge, Mass., 1962), 138.
7. Williams, "The Use of History", 110.
8. See, William M. Gibson, "Introduction" to *A Connecticut Yankee In King Arthurs Court* (New York, 1960) XVIII. Also see Deborah Berger Turnbull, "Hank Morgan as American Individualist", *Mark Twain Journal* 20, 1980 (2), 19-21; Nancy S. Oliver, "New Manifest Destiny in *A Connecticut Yankee in King Arthur's Court; Mark Twain Journal* 21, 1983 (4), 28-32; Charles S. Holmes, *"A Connecticut Yankee In King Arthur's Court; Mark Twain's* Fable of uncertainty", *South Atlantic Quarterly* 61, 1962 (Fall) 462-72; James J. Cox, *Mark Twain; The Fate of Humor* (Princeton, 1966), 203; David R. Swell, "Hank Morgan and the Colonization of Utopia", *American Transcendental Quarterly*, Mar. 1989, 3 (1), 27-44.
9. *Mark Twain's Letters,* ed. Albert Bigelow Paine (New York, 1917) II, 51.
10. Samuel Charles Webster, *Mark Twain, Business Man* (Boston, 1946), 335; *Mark Twain to Mrs. Fairbanks,* ed. Dixon Wecter (Sen Marino, Calif., 1949), 257.

11. *Mark Twain in Eruption* ed. Bernard Devoto (New York, 1940), 211.
12. Williams, "The Use of History", 103.
13. *Ibid.*, 102-10; 110.
14. Linda Hutcheon, *Poetics*, 24; see also XII, 16, 19-20.
15. *A Connecticut Yankee in King Arthur's Court* (New York; The New American Library; A Signet Classic, 1963), IX. All the references and page numbers are from this edition of the book.
16. Henry Nash Smith, *Mark Twain's Feble of Progress; Political and Economic Ideas* in "*A Connecticut Yankee*" (New Brunswick, N.J., 1964), 21.
17. *The Love Letters of Mark Twain* ed. Dixon Wecter (New York, 1949), 257-58.
18. Alfred Tennyson, "Ulysses", Line 4.
19. Lawrence 1. Berkove, "The Reality of the Dream : Structural and Thematic Unity in *A Connecticut Yankee". Mark Twain Journal* 22, 1984 (1) 10.
20. *Ibid.*, 9, 12.
21. *Ibid.*, 10.
22. *The English Historical Novels* (Baltimore, 1971), XII.

5

The Waste Land and *The Gita* : A Study in Spiritual Dynamics

DR. ANURAG SHARMA
Post Graduate Department of English
Dayanand (P.G.) College, Ajmer

Despite so much of spade-work done by scholars and researchers down the decades past, *The Waste Land* still remains an enigmatic poem. The enigma is due not only to the apparent complexity and obscurity pertaining to religio-mythical and literary allusions used so immensely by the poet but also to the inner complicated nature of the poem. "A heap of broken images" as the poem on first reading appears to be, it, nonetheless, is the poet's most successful attempt at finding some "metaphysical theory of the substantial unity of the soul...".[1] As a poet, Eliot could visualise that the panacea to the physical ailments of mankind lies not in physical things but in metaphysics. Like Gautam, the Buddha he seemed to have realised at the very outset that this world is a place of immense sorrow and misery—it is a Waste land—and he himself lived through the agony and the experience thereof for us—the waste-landers. He is with Wordsworth lamenting for what man has made of man.

No wonder, the *geisteswissenschaften* nature of Eliot's *Waste Land* exhibits his sincere concern and commitment to his contemporary world. It is an assimilative poem contentwise which is also apparent in the style of the poem—the assemblage, a kind of a patch-work and/or collage—of literary and classical allusions. The perspective is global and the perceptions of all times. As such, the poetic truth of the poem exists in a cosmic timelessness. It is here, at this particular juncture that I could find some common concerns which the poem seems to last phase, that had covered more than two decades, shows a mind accepting the idea of uncertainty and tentativeness, and toying with the various facets of the theme of unknowability. Since 1966 this new element, characterized also by a rejection of "modernism's high seriousness and hope for formal coherence and transcendence" (Bradbury 160) became increasingly obvious with each successive work. Greene had already been trying to grapple with a consciousness of uncertainties, indeterminacy of meanings and groping for an appropriate technique to express the same. This explains the uniqueness of his later works and especially the last two novels : *Monsignor Quixote* (1982) and *The Captain and the Enemy* (1988). (*Doctor Fischer* is rather a long short story, and *The Tenth Man* was written in 1944, through published...later). When *Monsignor Quixote* appeared, it was obviously striking in its freshness; it seemed to have no parallel in Greene's previous writing. The author used a completely new method here for his characters themes and narrative technique by interweaving the fictionality of the real with the reality of fictional (Allott[1]). The focus was on one Quixote who, again, was a 'descendant' of the Cervantes character and who was even befriended by one Zanchas on his journey along the same route in Post-France-Spain. The next novel, *The Capitan and the Enemy* had also once again startled the reader by apparently being a complete departure from whatever Greene had written earlier. Metaphorically speaking, what was earlier a planned journey along defined routes now turns into a 'journey without Maps' along the 'lawless roads' the vista of which has been opened before us by the post-modernist writings in English since, the late '60s. *The Capital and the Enemy* could indeed be studied as an example of what a post-modernist text could be in the hand of a writer like Greene. It exhibits, as it were, his own progress 'from work to text'. Its post-modernist features are only too overtly there to be missed. What Pynchon offered as the post-modernist fiction's penchant for abrupt transitions, comic book characters and melodramatic protting are only evident here. Even the language and style including sentence-structure remains tentative, never giving a finality of suggestion.

Apparently it is a most Dlippantly told brief tale of a casual writer, a young man of little education or achievement, who has decided to write something, and since he knows little else he writes about his own life starting as far back as he remembers. But even here he does not prove himself too much of a success. Neither the hero of Jim's proposed book, nor the author himself has fixed names. The 'main character', *i.e.*, the 'captain', undergoes innumerable shifts in name, role and identity, and one can never guess which is the true one. The same applies to a lesser degree to some other minor characters. Relationships too remain undefined : parent-child, friends-enemies, lovers-friends,—all relationships seem to get blurred and confusing. The child writer has two sets of parents, one original and the other adopted. To whom does he really belong? Or does he really belong to anyone? Who are friends and who are enemies. Again who are 'real friends' and who are just friends? These and similar questions are raised without any answer being given.

Greene's usual unencumbered racy style added to the overall jovial tone of the narration, makes enjoyable reading for a casual reader. But, at the same time, all along there are subtle undertones which pull a perceptive reader to various and contrary directions simultaneously. Too many incomplete sentences—sentences lacking closure and sentences paradoxically complete as well as incomplete—add to this indeterminacy the possibility of multiple interpretations. Words are frequently used to subvert the meaning by means of nonsense. It is such an indeterminacy that neither consistency nor certainty is possible. The text has to be read as an unknowable, unstable narrative. Through the apparent trivialization and carnival mood, a sense of alienation and sad vacuity percolates. Greene freely mixes the sublime and the ludicrous, the tragic and the comic, and harnesses language, vocabulary and syntax in a completely new way to create the suggestion that things "do (not) hold together". As result the book may be read, from beginning to end, like an unresolved riddle tempting one to infinite number of solutions and negating/counterbalancing each of them by some other solution no less/more valid at the same time.

II

M.K. Roy, in his article 'Two faces of Modernism' stresses 'unknowability' as one of the major aspects of post-modernism. A recognition of this element of unknowability may serve as starting paint for considering a discussion in postmodernism or a post-modernist text. As Bradbury says in his discussion of post-modernism in American novel, "all absolutes have become problematic" (162). It is perhaps interesting that apart from *The End of the Affair* (1951) *The Captain and the Enemy* is the only other book to introduce the narrator persona as an author or rather would-be author. Is it because the author as persona helps Greene to "question the act of imaginative writing at its heart" (Bradbury 164)?

Even as a small boy Baxter Jim (he has both the names) had nursed a secret ambition to be a writer one day : "I already had literary ambitions which I had not confided either to my aunt or my father" (32). He had read *King Solomon's Mines* four times and thought that if he ever went to Africa like his father "I would keep a journal of my adventures." (32)

Incidentally this is the only information he has of his father's movements, and the knowledge does not seem to improve till the end. In spite of being an 'author', he is helplessly ignorant, denied any kind of omniscience. He has to reconstruct the past by means of recollection, and even here he is not sure whether his memory proves true or false. He does not always know how to fill up the several gaps in this act of reconstructing the past or probing the characters. Victor Baxter-turned Jim, after being picked up from his school by the Captain, first arrives at London in the darkness of night. Getting up next morning "the strange events of the day before came trooping back to mind—I couldn't make sense of them, though I was quite happy...but I felt entirely lost in this new world" (36). This confusion, - inability to make sense and the sense of inexplicability of an absured nonsensical reality persists in his mind to the end. With a normal child's curiosity he asks Liza, his 'adopted mother', on the first morning about the 'Captain', regarding whom he practically knew nothing. But Liza stops him : "You are an inquisitive one...but don't go on like that with the Captain. Questions get him worried (37); and also hints at the impossibility of getting at the truth. At the child's query,—'Does he (the Captain) live here?' she makes a very evasive reply and knowing how enigmatic her reply sounds she adds : "When you get to know the captain better, you'll know that it's no good asking him questions. What he wants you to know, he'll tell you" (37). Yet she thinks it very important that Jim should know the Captain. "You've got to get to know the Captain" (43). But how to? It is as if she has known him. But has she? And could others get admitted into the mustery. There is no clue "It was as if for a moment she had let me into the important secret which would help to explain what was already a mysterious past and any future, equally mysterious, which was likely to come" (43). Later, as a young man of twenty-two Jim remembers "Both (Captain and Liza) of them were mysterious to me" (47). Jim here occupies the position that Alan Wilde cites as para-digmatic of the twentieth century artist, that of "the outsider, the uncommitted spectator, longing to overcome his self-consciousness, and make contact with the world outside his limited and limiting ego" (178).

The young man tries to piece up the broken fragments of a semi-forgotten past. Yet he knows that his account is not always exact : "I cannot pretend that all these details which I am trying so hard to reconstruct from my memory are necessarily true" (51), yet he is driven by a "compulsive passion"....to make these two people live before my eyes again, to bring them back out of the shadows and set them to play their sad parts as closely as possible of the truth" (91). At this point he makes an important confession : "I am only too well aware of how I may be weaving fact into fiction; but nevertheless, this is done "without an intention of betraying the truth". His supreme ambition is "to make the two of them clear to myself, so that they will continue to live as visibly as two photographs". At the same time he knows how impossible the task is of so comfortably grasping the 'mysterious'. In spite of realizing he cannot shake off his obsession with them which epitomises a writer's obsession with his characters. "Why am I so possessed by them? "Jim exclaims, and then he gives his own explanation. "It is as though I had taken them quite cold-bloodedly as fictional characters to satisfy this passionate desire of me to write" (51).

The difficulty of this reconstruction work which is continually haunted by the sense of 'mystery', the unknown, becomes apparent to the young writer at every step. As a child he had listened to a conversation between his original father and adopted mother, in which the 'signs' of language 'signified' nothing to the child. After so many years he is not sure if he can exactly remember the expression and mood which he had listened to without comprehending the language : "Their argument was quite beyond me in those days and it remained a mystery for many years, so that it was an argument meaningless to me then which I am trying to reproduce, and what I am writing now has to be based on my later knowledge" (56).

Again, as he tries to recall some of their simple, sparse conversation he knows his own inadequacy, but he cannot refrain from the attempt : "I don't pretend that I can remember correctly the details of this conversation. There are certain words which I do remember, but I invent far more of them, in order to fill in the gaps between their words," and his motivation is "to understand the only people in whom I could recognize...a kind of love".

The story is told in fragments, along whimsically ordained backward and forward courses through time (84). It seems to have been started when Jim was just a boy and then resumed after a long gap by the young man who accidentally comes upon the fragment : "There had been a period in my youth when I had nursed the vain ambition to become what I thought of as a 'real writer' and I suppose it was then that I began this fragment" (84). While rummaging among Liza's papers he reads the Captain's letter and an indomitable curiosity stirs within him. In order to have more information he meets the 'family Devil' : Perhaps it was the old ambition to be a 'real writer' which was latent in me and the curiosity of a would-be writer which drove me... (93), who is this 'real writer'? In Jim's mind this 'real writer' could give a good story with dependable details and a satisfactory conclusion. He goes to the Devil for information because "I want to continue this account and find a better conclusion than 'I wonder perhaps' " (93). As a 'real writer' he would have given a good conclusion after he had picked up and corrected the MS. "The end I could not foresee, ...I shall continue it and who knows what conclusion I may give it when I find myself with the Captain in that unknown territory of Panama" (106).

It is not only that Jim is uncertain about the end, he is uncertain about the very nature of his writing and at a loss how to define it. It is interesting to note the various names he attaches to it : "this draft—of what?" (84), "my own unfinished scrawl" (89), "this history" (105), "a journal" (106), "working on this old book of mine" (109), "fragment" (84), "this unfinished story—fiction, autobiography—which I have written here" (84), "this failed book of mine" (179), "all this scroll" (180). Towards the end, with the Captain's death, Jim stops writing, "I realize more than ever that I am no writer. A real writer's ambition does not die with his main character" (177). He says, "enough of all this nonsense" (179), and draws a line under the MS before throwing it into the waste paper basket, "the line means Finis" (180). Here is an example of "self-consciousness issuing in tremendous earnestness but also in far-reaching mockery", which Bradbury defines as a feature of post-modern novel (Bradbury 62). After his departure the colonel's people recover the papers and the colonel is also puzzled : "Shall I call it his novel? the colonel asks Mr. Quigly; the colonel assumes that 'king kong' is a code, though he fails to decode the sign : "how I would like to break that code of his !" (188) He even thinks of getting it published in Spanish, "Who knows it might even win a Cuban prize for the best work in gringo espionage" (188).

As a writer persona Jim is primarily concerned with restructuring the character of the so-called 'captain'. This is his obsession. But does he succeed? He knows so little about the man, and that little knowledge too is so riddled with enigmas, uncertainties. The man called 'Captain' remains a mystery to him as individual as well as in relation to others.

In Jim's lonely, neglected childhood birthdays went unremembered. The only birthday he remembers later was also the day when he first saw the Captain. The synchronization may suggest that meeting the Captain meant for him the start of a new life, a kind of rebirth. Yet, significantly, it was a "misty" day. And the mist covering the captain never lifts. Jim does not even know what his real name is : "The man, whom I would never come to know by any more permanent name than the Captain" (9-10). But the same morning the man signs the hotel bill as 'J. Victor (Capt.)'. The boy is rather surprised at the coincidence that his own name is also Victor, but also comforted by the feeling that "at last I had found a relative whom I could like" (17). On the way to Euston in the evening the boy asks because he has already some doubts "Is your name really Victor? His reply is worth noting : Oh, sometimes it's one thing and sometimes it's another. It wouldn't be much fun, would it, always carrying the same name from "birth till death" (21). According to this logic Victor Baxter too is readily changed into Jim and he is quite happy since "the possibility had never occurred to me of changing my hated name as easily as that just by choosing another" (28). The boy still wants to be sure how to address this man. He is told : "Just call me Captain unless I tell you different : There might come a time when I'd like to be addressed as Colonel—or Dad too might prove convenient—in certain situations" (21). The boy's curiosity, however, is not satisfied. So, next morning he tells Liza, 'It's funny. He has the same name as me" (*i.e.* Victor). Liza just says, "Oh, I suppose he borrowed it."

"Does he borrow a lot of names?" 'When I knew him first he had a very classy name—Colonel Claridge, but he changed that one pretty quick. He said he couldn't live up to it" (37). Now he is simply 'the Captain'. Liza hopes, 'That's a name...he'll always keep' (37-8) : Soon afterwards during one of the long spells of the Captain's absence, Victor's father pays a visit with reference to 'Roger's' postcard. He also insists that Roger had won his son from him in a game of chess, and not backgammon as he had told them; "Roger, you know, has a way of getting his details a little wrong. Even that name Captain which you call him. He was a sergeant not a Captain when the Germans were supposed to have nabbed him, and I doubt if they promoted him to an officer in captivity" (55). The last cheque Liza receives from him before she is taken to hospital is signed "for the time being by Carver,

(Because) I've never liked Cardigan—too honorifical—and I've had quite enough of Victor" (91). Following the clue of his last letter to Liza Jim reaches Panama to find the Captain again re-named. This time he is "Mr. Smith" (112). This time, of course, it's his "friends who have chosen the name...(as) they wanted something they could remember" (137). During his brief stay with the Captain in the Panama hotel Jim asks him : "Why did you keep on changing your name?" He offers an explanation, which is itself more a joke than an explanation : "It used to be more of a joke than serious in those days. Even when I was a small boy I always wanted to make fun of coppers. I don't like coppers" (137). The Captain's repeated renaming of himself may also suggest, besides the obvious explanation of situational exigency, a way of creating self-identity. Jim asks what name did he have when he was born. This shows Jim's attempt, futile though, to "get to know the Captain" (37) by taking a plunge backwards in time : The reply is : "My name was Browne" (137). Of course Jim is not convinced. The Captain's last letter to Jim before he takes his flight to death carries several signatures : "The Captain, the Colonel, the Major the Sergeant, Senor Smith with an exclamation mark after each name" (168). Why the exclamation marks? Do they mean fun, that he is neither of these persona, or is he all of them in one? Then why is his real name left out? Jim can only 'wonder' and 'suppose' (two words which pervade the texture of the novel) but cannot make out the man who had remained a "stranger" (11, 168) to him from first to last.

On his very first appearance the Captain carried an air of unreality, as if he were "an actor in costume", intended to play some role on the stage—an idea that gets pronounced since *The Comedians*. The idea that he has been acting roles (not one role) is suggested not only by his various appearances, but also by his behaviour, his mysterious ways, unpredictable dramatic and also sometimes stealthy appearances and disappearances. On their first meet the boy saw him winking, and he could hardly believe it since an adult was not supposed to wink at a child (10). It was as if the Captain with his "friendly, but unreliable eyes" (10) had been inviting the boy to share the fun of the comedy he has been acting, in which the bowler hat, the walking stick, carried like a mock-refle, the dyed hair, his moustache, beard are but part of his ever-changing costume. After years Jim would hesitate to say if the Captain was a good man (13) but he cannot downright condemn him either; the Captain remains the enigma. On their first acquaintance the Captain gives the hint that he has been around the world and so has learnt how to cheat people, in a small way, if necessary and also informs that often it so happens that he runs a bit short of cash (16). It is, as if, he is trying to prepare Jim for a new way of life, his way. Jim tries to guess his profession. "Are you a sea Captain ? But no, he said,...he was an army man" (17).

On a later occasion Jim's father says, "He has a lot of imagination" (55). Indeed this becomes evident from the very start in the quickness with which he fabricates stories about himself. In this sense he is also an author. First, he convinces the headmaster that he is "an old boy" though he has never been to the town before. Then he quickly assures the boy : "I don't always tell the exact truth. Any more than you do, I expect". He also advises him about the desirability to lie properly. "When I tell a lie no one can tell it from the gospel truth. Sometimes I can't even tell it myself" (20). Is it myth-making, the author being carried away by his own imagination about self? By evening they leave the hotel without paying the bills leaving behind an old suitcase with "a couple of bricks", yet when it comes to buying railway-tickets they have the entire compartment, because it is "essential" (22). Later the Captain drops hints about his past life, of a widely travelled man who has learnt from first-hand lessons of life. But are they true or false? Jim can never be sure, though he has a hunch that they are more fabricated than real. One of these stories is about his escape from a German prison camp and subsequent stay in the Spanish monastery. Jim will be realizing again and again what he had guessed at the beginning : "He's an awfully strange man" (34). Though he is pretty certain that as a boy he "liked the Captain", he still found him an "interesting" "mystery" (47).

Once, during those early days, he was excited at the possibility of solving the puzzle once, when the Captain had entrusted him with a newspaper and a message to Liza to read the second page. But he was disappointed to find nothing better than the story or a gang robbery. Jim could at best imagine, and not even guess where the Captain lived, or where he was at the moment, travelling, or in prison, or in pursuit of the legendary mules of Drake. And then suddenly after long intervals he would return in another stage costume, a tall bearded Captain, wielding his stick like a weapon and equipped with a car; the beard would disappear again within a week and the next time he returns with a moustache in a different style and colour (70).

The Captain's method of teaching Jim Geography and history is also quite interesting and original showing the creative mind of an imaginative writer. "They were lessons drawn from the experience of a traveller in rather unusual circumstances and perhaps they were more vivid than the superficial second-hand knowledge of a school teacher" (62). These lessons are naturally an enjoyable game for the boy, because they are little more than stories, and the stories also undergo variations depending on the occasion and the auditor. "The details did not always tally" (67) Jim, Liza, and Quigly are also actors, though of a much lover order, playing their respective roles in the 'comedy' of life.

Again, in a way, both Jim and the Captain are authors, fabricating their respective stories through the complex memory game of retention and rejection. As Jim says : "I am doing my best to describe a lesson which I received from the Captain, but I realize only too well that my description cannot be factually accurate. It has passed through the memory and the memory rejects and alters much as the Captain may have changed a lot of facts when he recounted his wartime experiences. The boy has a suspicion that with Liza in his audience "he wanted to make the story a bit more interesting (and) perhaps...he may deliberately lie a little" (67). So it is like the creative writer who is under the obligation to make his story more interesting and so fall in for the fictional in preference to the real or was there really any such demarcation line between the fictional and the real?

During his twelve hour journey from Amsterdam to Panama Jim works on the Ms, and once again realizes how the enigma named the Captain, has haunted him all these years and still remains inexplicable : "If it were possible for the Captain to read what I am writing now he would learn how much I have continued to wonder about him—he is to me an eternal question mark never to be answered, like the existence of God, and so, as all theologians do, I continue to write in order to turn the question over and over without any hope of an answer" (109). Who is the Captain, and who is/are his enemy/ enemies remain undefined enigmas.

Jim cannot, indeed, reconcile the various angles which have been brought to bear upon the Captain. According to the Devil he is little more than "a liar and a crook" the dangerous underground type, and "yet it was on this liar and crook that Liza and I had depended for years, and not once had he ever finally failed us" (110). He had absurdly enough won the boy in a game of backgammon; yet "he was the nearest thing I had known to be what I thought of as a father" (110). Though overtly a reckless cheat, Liza acknowledges him all along till her last letter as the "kindest" man she has ever known. Towards the end, waiting for the Captain, in the continental Hotel of Panama he acknowledges, "I felt as though I were waiting for a stranger", and it was in vain that "I had tried to recreate this character in my sorry attempt to become a 'real writer' (126). Thus Jim's tentative memoir suggests the possibility of any number of names—identities—adventures, which the Captain had might have had/imagined/fabricated,—that interpretations based on these elements are effectively pre-empted or nullified and the text subverts/undermines regular reading conventions like interpretation, gap-filling, assemblage.

Jim also tries to fabricate lies; but he is found out. Apparently he is not as good a story-teller as the Captain. In many ways Jim plays the second fiddle to the Captain. Even as a child he had been an 'Amalekite'—an alien pursued by the 'enemies'; the Captain is also identified with a hunted 'King Kong' who cannot shirk his burden of love and is in search of some just republic. For Jim, the boy, knowledge evades him regarding the question of self-identity. He feels lost in his "new world" because, "at the age I was then, a boy doesn't give as much importance to happiness as to knowing who he really is" (36).

As an adult he tries to identify the Captain's identity, but he evades comprehension. Both dream of their own respective "mule bells". The Captain is also a prolific better writer, who often uses words not as familiar signs, but to signify something else than the dictionary meaning. And Jim wonders : "Can it be from the Captain I have somehow inherited this irritating desire to be a writer. It certainly wasn't from the Devil or from my mother.... Didn't I a bit resemble, in my desire to find words, the Captain in his perpetual search for mules which carried gold" (140)?

The Captain also searches for words to express his exact feelings. And these words are sometimes startling in their apparent inappropriateness; often these are absurdly out of place, signs which faintly signify a suggestion or are completely devoid of signification yet this is part of his style. Listening to it for the first time the boy is puzzled. The Captain suggests that Jim could all Liza 'Mum". Jim protests : 'But she's not my mother'. And he is assured in reply, "Mother is just a generic term". "What's generic? I think he took a pleasure in using difficult words—a sort of showing off, but there was more to it than that I learned latter" (26) what is this 'more'. Does the captain enjoy evasion or is it an artistic necessity on his part? During one of their fantastic geography lessons Jim asks "what's partugal like?", and gets the answer : "An agglomeration of sardines" (65). He used words which I doubt if either of us really understood. Once while shaving off his unaccustomed beard (another act of changing costume) the captain cuts himself : " 'I never feel at home in this thing', he told me. It always reminds me of those fuliginous days in the Pyrenees, no chance of saving there" (68). Now Jim knows him more to be upset by 'fuliginous'. In a later letter to Liza he writes : "the hair is beginning to go. I'll soon be glabrous. It's always that way when I'm without you", Jim, going through this letter, wonders "what the hell did 'glabrous' mean. I looked it up in a dictionary when I got back to my room and found as the answer 'smooth skinned'. It made some sense for once unlike most of the long words he liked to use" (88). But how far does the dictionary meaning really fit in the context? Anyway, in a later sequence when the Captain uses the word once again, Jim cannot make sense. As Jim writes his phoney telegram asking an imaginary friend for information about Liza's sickness (a woman already dead), the Captain suggests the message "could be a bit more glabrous" and Jim realizes, "That word bore for him a large variety of meanings which were unknown to me" (151). In another letter he mentions his dream about Liza's accident as "this funambulist dream" (90). Jim looks up 'funambulist' too in the dictionary. "I think he must have connected it with words like 'funeral' and 'funereal', for the true meaning 'rope-walker' certainly made no sense" (90). Saying one thing to mean something quite other has been perhaps basic to the Captain's survival as a hunted man, though Greene's other 'hunted men' who have been appearing in his novels since 1929, do not show this zest for word-play. Jim concludes : "He was not so educated as Liza thought" (90). However, in another letter the Captain informs that he takes only whisky now since "tea which reminds me of you seems a bit too funambulist (92). The same words seems to simultaneously trace and erase various meanings. Regarding his choice of the name (temporary of course) Carver, he explains; "I've never liked Cardigan—too honorifical" (91). The Captain's only letter inviting Liza to join him in Panama says : "Come quickly and made Carver goluptious" (94). In the Panama hotel, Jim wakes up one morning to find a brief note : "I shall be back before dark, just a short fuliginous flight" (139). By this time Jim is so worked up with guilt and envy that the word fails to amuse him. "Even the Captain's misuse of that absurd word fuliginous irritated me" (139). In his irritation Jim even shows to Quigly, the 'financial correspondent' for an American magazine, who is expectedly puzzled. " 'What on earth does fuliginous mean?' Mr. Quigly asked. 'I knew once, but I've forgotten. I don't carry a dictionary around. Anyway a dictionary wouldn't help. I think he cares only for the sound. He gets the meanings wrong' " (139). As a hunted man, the Captain is necessarily an outsider to this society. Thus in his usage the words on which the accepted dictionaries/society have one meaning reinscribe those same signs and have them signify some other undefined thing. Is this one of his ways to overcome/evade the society? Jim even tells Quigly the story the Devil had told him about the half-destroyed dictionary, the only book the Captain could lay hand on during imprisonment. Is it the reason for his odd words beginning not alphabetically lower than 'h'. Jim tries to explain : "He doesn't often use words like that when he speaks, but they seem to get control when he writes" (140), and Quigly comments : 'Like a Poet?'

It is, again, remarkable how incomplete sentences abound in the text. It is left for the reader to fill up the gap. Yet it is impossible for the reader to fill in the gap because there are so many equally valid or not so valid possibilities, reminding one of Barthes's *S/Z.* To cite a few examples :

On their first arrival at Euston the Captain and the boy walk home when he asks if Jim remembered his mother, and then says "Your father told me...but he never said what it was that my father had told him" (23). For a child the adult world and its ways are normally inexplicable to some extent. Thus beginning the novel with a child narrator could prove a clever device to register the enigma of life. When the Captain brings home a real child to spring his surprise on Liza, she is scared : "I never meant you to do anything when I said...I just thought...if only things had been different..." (29), a sentence broken into three parts each of which remains incomplete. Later the Captain tells the boy confidentially, "I want her to forget". He repeated, "to forget..." (42). But to forget what? The 'devil'? Her past? Her inability to bear a child? Her loneliness? The gap is not filled up.

When the boy's infuriated aunt wants to check the credentials of the Captain as teacher, he simply says 'Call me Captain' (73) but does not satisfy her curiosity any further, as if the title Captain includes either name or qualification or both, Chapter six ends with an incomplete sentence. Jim thinks of the odd pair, Captain and Liza, whom he had less than half known in his childhood : "I have always wondered if perhaps...(79). Chapter seven begins with the same retrospective tone : "I have always wondered". Then Jim questions himself : "What was it that I 'always wondered', I ask myself as I read this account of our life together, an account which I had begun to write years before".

But after all these years still "I found no answer to my question in it" (83). When the Devil warns him about fooling the Captain ("He's an underground type",) Jim just says "All the same..." (102) and leaves his speech incomplete. The phrase "all the same" suggests a counterpoint. Does he refuse to frame the captain in a particular type, or does he send the signal that he will go ahead in spite of risks. This innocuous phrase could be interpreted in many ways. After the Captain's sudden last flight. Jim is called to the Colonel's office; because "We wondered if perhaps he (Quigly) said a word to you which might indicate..." (171). But indicate what? Betrayal? Danger? Wrong direction? Escape? Death? Murder? Any interpretation may be derived by the reader. But the author gives no certain or definite answer. At the end Quigly is served the notice to leave the native zone of Panama though what me may have done is "of little concern now, except..." (186). Except what? That remains a riddle.

An abundance of this sort of incomplete sentences imparts to the narration an air of tentativeness which is further underscored by questions to one's one self and to others—which are raised but left unanswered. The young man tries to recapture his childhood emotions in terms of a series of questions : "Did I miss him? ...Had I grown to love the Captain? ....Did I love Liza?...Did I love anyone? Did I know what love was? Do I know it now years later or is love something which I have read about in books" (77-78). He cannot answer any of these questions definitely. Neither is he any better in seeing through others. As he rummages through the Captain's letters to Liza, "In search of knowledge" he remembers his father's talk about the Captain's lies. "But what, I asked myself, had the Captain to gain from lying to Liza when he was so far away? What relationship could remain intact when two thousand miles intervened? Why keep up such a comedy? Or was it a comedy which the Captain was playing to himself alone to escape from his loneliness." (91)? When Colonel Martinez informs Jim that Mr. Smith has been seen flying off in a different direction than "he had been ordered to take" Jim makes a question "Vulgarly direct" : "Who gave him the order? You or Mr. Quigly?" But even this direct question gets no answer. The talk is diverted to Quigly.

The extraordinary frequency (an interested reader may take a count) of words and phases like "I think", "I suppose", "I believe", "perhaps", "anyway", "I wondered" may be seen in the light of this overall tentativeness. To cite just two examples : "What work? I wondered. The word 'wonder' seemed to come only too often to my mind" (92).

Again, as the Devil tries to decipher the Captain's letter—"I think he thinks...", Jim feels : "It seemed to me that one 'think' almost immediately gave birth to another 'think'. 'Thinks' were breeding like rabbits—or that other word 'wonder' " (101).

The syntax of a large number of sentences is also determined by this tentativeness which percolates through the confusing arrangements of 'yet', 'or', 'if', 'but', 'perhaps' within a single sentence or passage.

Waking up in the empty room of the Panama hotel Jim finds the Captain's letter to Liza still there "perhaps because he meant to continue it after his work—what work?—the next evening or not send it at all" (131). He fails to understand the anxiety of the Colonel and Quigly over the Captain's absence : "hadn't his life been full of absences since that first absence of his from the German Camps...if the story he told me was true? Did Mr. Quigly and the Colonel fear a betrayal, *but* wasn't his life full of betrayals? He had pretended to love Liza and yet he had left her continually, ..." (173). In the long years of his lonely boyhood Jim had to get accustomed, like Liza, to the many unpredictable absences of the Captain. Indeed, the story is premised on the absence of certainty, security, home, parents (both original and adopted), even the absence of an adequate language. Thus long series of suggestions would be immediately undermined by counter suggestions. At the end Jim ponders alone what to do : "The Captain would have advised me from his own experience, *but* he's safe and dead, and *anyway* would I have trusted him? It was only for Liza that he cared *if* he ever cared for her...*perhaps* I have never understood the nature of love. *Perhaps*...I wish I had seen him once more *or* that I hadn't lied to him..." (178-79).

The language here is symptomatic of "the post-modernist text which systematically unmakes itself even as it goes on making itself up" (C.D. Malmgren). The language of the text, indeed, seems to simultaneously construct and dissolve structures both linguistic and thematical. The element of tentativeness that qualifies the syntax pattern, language and method of story-telling, suggests a connection between Greene's narrative strategy (at its maturest) and the epistemological realities of modern life, its facelessness, namelessness, rootlessness, instability, uncertainly, and ingrained unknowability.

It is perhaps only befitting that such a book should end too with a question mark, and even this last question ("The vital question remains—what or who is King Kong?" (180) should be an ironically misplaced emphasis which is unlikely to yield any satisfactory answer. Thus *The Captain and the Enemy* assumes a postmodernist position which finds expression in the complex and decentered form and language of a post-modern novel.

NOTE

1. "His (Greene's) novels span the long period from the fag-end of modernism in the thirties, through the revival of documentary realism in the fifties, to the indulgence in narrative games about the fictionality of the real and the reality of fiction which have become familiar to us since the sixties."—M. Allott, 'Surviving The Course, Or a Novelist for all Seasons : Graham Greene's *The Honorary Consul,*' *The Uses of Fiction,* (Ed. D. Jefferson, G. Martin) (Stratford : The Open University Press, 1982).

WORKS CITED

Barthes, R., *S/Z* (Tr. Richard Miller), New York : Hill and Wang, 1974.

Bradbury, M., *The Modern American Novel,* (1983), New York : Oxford University Press, 1984.

Couto, M., *Graham Greene : On the Frontier.* London : The Macmillan Press Ltd., 1988.

Greene, G., *The Captain and the Enemy* (1988), New York : Penguin Books, 1989.

Malmgren, Carl D., 'From Work to Text : The Modernist and Post-modernist Künstlerroman' *Novel,* Vol. 21, No.1, Fall, 1987.

O'Prey, P., *A Reader's Guide to Graham Greene,* Worcester : Thames and Hudson, 1988.

Ray, Mohit K., 'Two Faces of Postmodernism', *Critical Practice,* (Vol I, No. 1), New Delhi : *Creative Books,* Winter, 1994.

Wilde, A., *Horizons of Assent : Postmodernism and the Ironic Imagination,* Baltimore : John Hopkins University Press, 1981.

6

To Be and To Choose : Ken Kesey's *Sometimes a Great Notion*

MS. P. SHAILAJA
Kakatiya University, Warangal

> "My book is trying may be too Goddam much, trying to encompass a man, a family, a town, a country and a time—all at once, simultaneously and work them into a story and have the story say something important, Awful much, Awful much."

This is indeed Ken Kesey's great notion about his *Sometimes a Great Notion*. Drawn from his working notes[1] these lines evidently signify that this novel of Kesey has been a product of his ambitious venture. It is more ambitiously conceived and executed than his earlier book *One Flew Over the Cuckoo's Nest*. The comprehensiveness of the novel manifests itself in its length, the number of characters and the frequent shifts in time and person. The multiple perspectives which the novel unfolds account for its rich complexity.

The different levels of inference in the novel may be analysed metaphysically as the novel shows the absurdity of human quest in a meaningless universe, the insignificance of human endeavour and its struggle against a natural world; and psychologically since it reveals the ramifications of an oedipal situation in which Hank's affair with his stepmother over-shadows Lee's life. The historical aspect reveals the frontier successes and failures and how the memory of Hiroshima destroys heroic potential. The social concern reveals that modern reality is determined by technological and organizational phenomena. In the rigid organizational set-up, the 'collective man' at once opposes and admires individualism.

Kesey's intention is not a simple presentation of the inferences in order to uphold some truths and reject a few others. In fact his treatment of these truths has been found by Stephen L. Tanner[2] to be 'vague and tenuous' while Leslie Fiedler[3] dubbed it a 'strained effort'. But it cannot be denied that Kesey was grappling with these truths to find the meaning of life and the values needed to sustain it. Ronald G. Billingsley[4] uses the image of a 'Spoked wheel' to explain Kesey's technique and it can with equal success be applied to his thematic organization, where each spoke represents an ideological truth and the rim is the life which absorbs all these truths and becomes something different. Kesey gives force to this idea in the novel when he says "Reality is greater than the sum of its parts, also a damn sight holier."[5]

Kesey believes that most people are involved and trapped in a reality they are not even aware of. Time, place and people may shape character and determine destinies. But it is a human-being who has to rely on his 'individual sanity' and find meaning and values in life. As he often says, "What this Country needs is sanity, Individual sanity, and all the rest will come true".[6] Since no philosophical truth for him is complete and all inclusive, *Sometimes a Great Notion* works out the thesis directing the readers to 'look, pay attention', in order to understand this.

An attempt is made here to study the historical and the social. Kesey feels that man should not allow himself to be trapped by external realities, but he should use his sanity to find a meaningful existence. The novel elucidates this truth by creating Hank and Lee as complementary characters ideologically and temperamentally, who in the end acquire an all inclusive view of life. Hank a frontier individual is in contrast to Lee a product of mass society. Hank stands for courage and Lee for temerity, Hank's gusto for life and Lee's fear of it; Hank's fortitude and Lee's clandestine plan for revenge; Hank's physical and psychological tiredness and Lee's puny self-pity; Hank's belief in strength and Lee's refuge in weakness vividly come to the fore in the novel. It is in the interaction with each other and with the external manipulative forces that both Hank and Lee become conscious of their own inadequacies and painfully accept the necessity to develop more fully as human beings by changing their preconceived notions of themselves.

Sometimes a Great Notion opens with a grotesque symbol hanging from a pole at the Stamper house. This is old Henry's amputated arm, fist up with all but the middle finger tied down. The union and the town's people gathering on the other side of the river are shouting and booing at Hank. The hand stands in silent defiance to all this commotion. The collective force of the union and the individualistic action of Hank stand opposed. The entire novel is an unfolding of the incidents leading to Hank's present gesture.

The frontier as a geographical and economic entity had vanished from the American continent with the statement made by the Superintendent of the census in 1890 that "The free lands have gone, the frontier has vanished." But F.J. Turner[7] has pointed out that life in America has been conditioned by the perennial rebirth of frontier manifested in man's attempt to "control nature, industry and his own self." The frontier man displayed a pioneering spirit—

> a spirit of determination, of endurance, of independence, of ingenuity, of flexibility, of individualism, of optimism.[8]

These traits have influenced American psyche and moulded its character. Henry and Hank are the products of frontier spirit.

Jonas Stamper a restless west-walker, comes along with his sons to Oregon from Kansas pursuing the dream of conquering new frontiers. He settles down on the banks of Wakonda Auga, begins a big house and believes that this new frontier would make him feel big and be big. But he is soon intimidated by the country and feels small and insignificant. Back in Kansas he is responsible for the life around him. If he does not water the crops they fail, if he does not feed the stock, the stock dies. But here the flora and fauna grow or die in complete disregard and he is overawed by the natural world. His house becomes a prison to him and one night he walks out and returns to Kansas. Jonas is an average man, less confident of his success, and Kesey shows in him that for one superman who succeeds there are a hundred average men who fail. There are also other pictures of frontier people who are too shiftless, too passionate, as in the images of the bolt-cutter and Ben's father.

Jonas's son Henry is filled with a restless, nervous energy. He takes charge of the family and begins the long struggle against life and society. He is repeatedly warned that a man cannot live and work by himself. The co-operative society in the name of safety and security, advocates togetherness and collective effort. But Henry believes that its membership would force him to bow to its dictates and deprive him of his freedom, and he sets out to prove that he can succeed all alone. He imbibes the pioneering spirit, completes the home, builds the logging business and becomes "the calm, stubborn, confident rock of a man" (468)—a true pioneer.

Hank is the quintessential of Stampers. Henry, his father instills his philosophy of "Never Give a (Sic) Inch" into Hank. He grows into a tough, stubborn, self-reliant individual. He becomes "one of the ten toughest hombres west of the Rockies" (105). He acquires bobcats at odds, fights bears, establishes records in wrestling, swimming and football, relies on his strength and upholds western values. The river becomes a force he has to constantly fight against. It erodes his land and threatens him with defeat and death. Like his father he begins the long struggle of preservation by shoring up the foundation with timbers and cables. Preserving the house is preserving his life against defeat and death. Hank believes that to stop fighting means to start dying. To him a man with a spine is a man able to live, however difficult it may be and he believes that "If you want to win, you does your best". One's best is "going after it with everything you got, fighting and kicking, stomping and gouging, and cussing it when everything else went sour" (105).

Hank unlike his father (who was a true pioneer in word and deed) at times feels weary and isolated. He suppresses this as he is made to reveal only the strong face to the world. The words of his grandfather "lessed are the meek..." on the plaque have a braille-effect on him and mould his responses.

Hank's will to live is achieved through defiance. But simultaneously his yearning to give up the struggle, lose his identity and become a part of the crowd is also evident. That Kesey wanted to emphasize this conflict is apparent in the following lines which preface the novel :

> "Sometimes I live in the country,/Sometimes I live in the town,/Sometimes I get a great notion/To Jump into the river ...an' drown."

The river is a symbol not only for the natural force but also for the collective human forces. It stands as a metaphor for "the confluence of many individual lives into a turbulent society, many voices into one chorus".[9] Kesey makes this conflict of frontier individualism and dissolution in the crowd, central to Hank's realisation of the meaning of life and its values. And this is brought to a head in his fight with Lee and the union.

Kesey alludes to the post-world war II society in which the memory of the bombing of Hiroshima offers constant pain. "That mighty first boom was only the first faintest murmer of an explosion that is still roaring down on us, and always will be" (505). These memories undermine the heroic, pioneering spirit. Hank, returning from the war, discovers a bland despair in his people. They seemed "tired, scared and asleep" (105). Instead of living with 'style and grit' they are living passively, and now he is threatened by the collective organizational values.[10] Hank's decision to supply Wakonda pacific with logs and not be bound by the Union's decision is resented by the union and the town's people.

Draeger is a perfect spokesman of organizational values. He is essentially a manipulator. His movements are calculated. He never loses temper and cultivates a soothing patience in his voice which is almost mesmerizing. To him the world is simple, precise rational and predictable. Man is not unique, but a conditioned commodity, whose responses can be foreseen. He jotted down notes in his little book, reducing life to neat little phrases. He has a 'package of truths' about men and their actions formed over a span of twenty five years of his experience in labour and management and he had been using this knowledge as a weapon for twenty five years with success.

Teddy like Draeger manipulates others with his quiet confident, superior intelligence. Evenwrite is conditioned by psychological forces he does not understand. He is intellectually and temperamentally unsuited for the white-collar job. He is confused and unhappy in his role, but is nonetheless incapable of freeing himself from it. Boney Stokes, Les Gibbons, Big Newton, Willard Eggleston are shaped by the pre-determined identity pressed on them. The collective society never allows a person to think and act independently. And as such, he feels he is not responsible for his state but throws the blame on others :

> "Oh, me the trouble such, oh my the trouble is so, the trouble is the ra-dio, the trouble is the republicans, the trouble is the Democrats, the trouble is the communists..." (94).

Lee, Hank's half-brother is a product of the collectivist society. Lee grows into a neurotic and a cynic as he feels that Hank has robbed him of his mother, by his physical possession of her. As a regaining tactic, he attempts to win her by his weakness and lures her away to New York, but lives under this emotional disturbance ever afterwards. He accuses Hank of depriving him of a sense of self. His mother made him believe that the river and mountains were walls. He fears to love, to care for others as that would leave him vulnerable to pain. There is a constant inner voice of fear, which warns him to 'watch out'.

Throughout his life, Lee avoided his responsibility of coping with his own problems and blamed for their origin on others :

> "It was my brother Hank; it was my ancient fossil of a father who frightened and disgusted me, it was my mother whose name be frailty...they were the ones who tore my young life asunder" (217).

Lee is more like Teddy and Draeger in his sly methods and manipulation. When he fails to measure upto Hank, he plans to pull him down and does not hesitate to use his weakness as a weapon.

The contrast between the brothers comes out clearly in their relation to 'Viv', Hank is too strong to need anyone, imposes his will on her and does not perceive her true self. Lee uses her as a weapon to further his revenge and trics to win her with his weakness, "look Viv, look at Lee needing so much, see how he is so small in the word". (269)

The Union, towns people and Lee blame Hank for their misfortunes. There is fear, inaction, cowardly blaming in their actions. Evenwrite repeats that these times demand sacrifice on the part of the individual. Draeger argues from a national perspective and when this fails, he starts his usual tactics of manipulation. He talks with the people in the town and very skillfully makes them form a group[11] and act according to group wishes. He articulates and justifies their resentment. He kindles the vision of a breathtaking future so as to justify the sacrifice of a transitory present. He stages the world of make-believe, so indispensable for the realization of self-sacrifice and united action. He picturises individual existence to be petty and meaningless. He isolates Hank and applies psychological pressure.

Hank feels that he is being deprived of his independent judgement and free choice. He feels that his life is being challenged and as a firm believer in Stamper ethic does not believe in weakness. By standing on his word, he proves his belief in his own capacity to make meaningful choices and thus resist the collective forces. He knows he is risking total alienation of the town's people and will also be losing his wife, if he undertakes to deliver the logs. But if he does not fulfil his contract "he may lose his life" (12).

Hank becomes a superhuman to prove his strength. On the last day the incidents move swiftly. Hank, tired, vulnerable lapses from his responsibility of choice under Henry's leadership. As Leeds comments :

> "He has in his exhaustion, abdicated his responsibility to lead, to think as a human being. Instead he is satisfied to drive himself as a machine, under another's directions".[12]

After Ben's death, when he returns dead tired, beaten by union things, swimming the river, he finds Viv and Lee in a sexual embrace. The physical and mental tension beat him and he sinks thinking : "No, there ain't any true strength-there's just different degrees of weakness..." (500). He feels isolated from the universe and from the mankind as well. On the day of Joe Ben's funeral, the sun is unusually bright. To Hank, the sun's bright glare like that of the atom bomb, shines on a world denuded of life and meaning. His illusions about strength disintegrate.

Hank despairs. But Lee's influence helps him to step out of this subjectivity. His confidence in his strength is restored when Lee for the first time turns back and fights him. It affords a richer and fuller view of life. He discovers an underlying weakness within his strength and realizes a greater depth in life. His definition of strength becomes comprehensive. As Leeds says of him :

> "Not merely sensitivity and cerebration but humility and even the admission of weakness are necessary, as Hank ultimately realizes to the development of a man. Yet the awareness of one's vulnerability does not obviate the moral responsibility to make meaningful choices in one's life and by acting upon them, to define oneself existentially. These realizations are a long time in coming to Hank, given the rigidity of the stamper ethic transmitted to him by his father."[13]

His strength restored, he decides to show to others that he will oppose "everything except a hand extended." He is ready to face every hazard, lay down his life, endure pain and ridicule, but will "relinquish his firmest stand for love" (2) and decides to fulfil his contract though alone.

Hank's actions force Lee to learn the truth about life. He understands the importance of love and one's capacity to respond to it. He recognizes that he cannot live fully by ignoring the reality and his personal responsibility for his present state. He learns that to regain power over his life he must recapture the ultimate sovereign right to choose his values, for surrendering this right for any reason other than love is surrendering love.

Draeger and Teddy discover greater forces, which they don't understand "there are bigger forces, Mr. Draeger. I don't know what they are, but they get ours whipped sometimes" (597).

Hank's actions virtually force all to come to terms with their illusions and preconceived notions.

Animal and tree imagery illuminate his theme. Kesey uses animal nature to probe human nature. Hank is like the "lone goose" and Lee as a victim is a 'fox running for its life', and when seeking revenge on Hank, friendship and sex with Viv is a 'cunning fox' Hank's special dog Molly, pursues the bear despite loneliness and danger, like Hank pursuing independence and self-reliance despite social alienation. The union and the towns people are like the pack of dogs who feel safe in numbers. As the snake strikes Molly out of self-preservation, so also the union members subotage Hank's operation to safeguard their jobs. The tree imagery also reveals collective or individual character. To the union the trees are simply a source of income. To Jonas the forest is a place of death and destruction. To Henry and Hank it is a challenging and worthy opponent bringing out the best in them. To Lee the frost and the river are walls.

To convey the total reality of an event, Kesey used multiple points of view and freedom from sequential time. He attempts to express the complex subjective aspects of life. The novel covers the happenings of a single day. But in order to understand the events and characters, the reader has to understand many other things—about the Stamper house and the family tradition, about Myra, about the union and towns people. It requires the reader to put the parts together and perceive them as a whole. The theme is a single event, but at the same time is composed of dozens of evens all being narrated simultaneously. In addition to all the voices there is also the author's voice omnipresent, which introduces the chapters, comments, philosophises and establishes the unity of dissimilar elements. Kesey's technique reveals the complexity of the actual world.

Hank and Lee represent Kesey's hope for future. Armed with love and understanding they can escape the society functioning as an institution and dedicate themselves to a free life.

NOTES

1. Quoted by Stephen L. Tanner, *Ken Kesey* (Boston : Twayne, 1983), p. 53.
2. Tanner, *Ken Kesey.*
3. Leslie Fiedler, *The Return of the Vanishing American* (New York : Stein and Day, 1968).
4. Quoted by Tanner, p. 59.
5. Ken Kesey, *Sometimes a Great Notion* (New York : Viking, 1964), p. 14. All parenthetical references in the text hereafter are from this edition.
6. Ken Kesey, *One Flew Over the Cuckoo's Nest,* ed. John Clark Pratt (New York : Viking, 1973), p. 12.

7. F.J. Turner, "The Significance of the Frontier in American History," *American Reader*, ed. M. Thomas Inge (New Delhi, 1989), pp. 80-87.
8. Lucy Lockwood Hazard, *The Frontier in American Literature* (California, 1927), p. xviii.
9. Gilbert M. Porter, *The Art of Grit : Ken Kesey's Fiction* (Columbia : University of Missouri Press, 1982), p. 42.
10. William H. Whyte, *The Organisation Man* (New York : Simon, 1956), p. 57.
11. Speaking about the formation of groups, Eric Hoffers says : "They are eager to barter their independence for relief from the burdens of willing, deciding and being responsible for inevitable failure. They will abdicate the directing of their lives to those who want to plan, command and shoulder all responsibility," in *The True Believer* (New York : Harper, 1951), p. 109.
12. Barry H. Leeds, *Ken Kesey* (New York : Ungar, 1981), p. 78.
13. *Ibid.*, p. 61.

7

Deconstructing History : A Study of Mahasweta's *Imaginary Maps*

PROF. A. JAGANMOHANA CHARI
Department of English
Kakatiya University, Warangal

Mahasweta Devi's absolutization in geometrical terms of no-meeting point between the tribals and the mainstream signifies the space and time of post-Independence India fictionally sited in *Imaginary Maps* which is dedicated by the novelist, 'for all the indigenous peoples of the world', translated by Gayatri Chakravorty Spivak into English and published by Thema, Calcutta 1993. The historical specificity of the statement made by the activist-novelist :

> The tribals and the mainstream have always been parallel. There has never been a meeting point.
>
> (Mahasweta Devi : ii)

to Gayatri Spivak brooks a post-modernist version of the negation of human practice.

Mahasweta's statement textualizes itself as a metaphysically conceived fact which is out of the bounds of the dialectic of history, *i.e.*, change. It is noteworthy here that Gayatri Spivak characterizes, in another context, Mahasweta's fiction as "history imagined into fiction" (95) (which may serve incidentally as a facile generalization for all post-modernist fiction). If it is so, it may call for a question : how come Mahasweta thinks as an activist in terms of metaphysics which admits no change and writes fiction which is 'imagined' history whose cardinal principle is change. One answer for this question could be the assumption that her activist statement is engendered by a mood of desperation. But this assumption in my opinion will certainly make light of her fiction undeservedly. But the hiatus in this context can also be attributed to the self-devouring or negativistic tendency implicit in post-modernism *a la* Derrida, the influence of which Gayatri Spivak discovers in Mahasweta's fiction (Blurb to *Imaginary Maps*). But more importantly, one can credit Mahasweta with a clarity of vision which comes to an historically informed realist with a concern for the marginalized people in the world, the indigenous and the disenfranchised or the deprivileged.

The logocentric universe the human race has inherited has as its corner stone the hierocratic or hierarchical value-system, as structuralist and post-structuralist thinkers including Derrida have demonstrated. Somewhere along the line, Manichean dichotomies-binary in character but hierarchical in value—came to constitute the core or the center of metaphysics of presence as being, in the West. This center of metaphysics of presence as being is central to all Western philosophical systems, down the ages, Derrida argues (Jaques Derrida : 298). In brief, the dialectic of domination or hegemony seems to have become a cardinal principle of life in the West. This may very well explain the lop-sided dichotomous pairs or opposites which have plagued the Western tradition. Controversies about free-will vs. destiny during the medieval times, nature vs. the world in the Romantic era and man vs. woman in the modern times could be cited as cases in point here.

I am not concerned here with giving a theoretical explanation of the modernist movements of resistance arising in the context of Western tradition. What I wish to highlight is the logic or dialectic behind the habit of domination of Western tradition or Western mores which, when come into contact with the pre-capitalist or pre-feudal modes of lived life, mercilessly trampled them into submission or destroyed them. This, I think, explains the disastrous colonial expropriation and imperialist exploitation of the third world countries by the West. It is also not my intention to devaluate the role and dimension of historical materialist dialectic in this process, but only to valorize the metaphysically-given ontological status of Western modes of thought or values like reason, will, ego, violence, and pleasure which together constitute power—power to impose oneself on others. It is this power, or desire to power, or to dominate by imposing one's will on others which characterize all Western ideals and practices including the imitative or borrowed ones on the part of post-colonial neo-colonials like Indian upper-castes. It is this violence-packed dichotomous relation which inflates or privileges one member as the prime one and deflates or disenfranchizes the other instead of sublating both in a dialectical unity. This is what has been obtained as the ontological condition of life of the Western-modernist-capitalist-bourgeoisie and that of its post-colonialist third world epigoni. The disenfranchized member—whether it is a woman or man—in this synchronically witnessed ontological reality with a built-in series or codes of relations which are inexorably oppressive, is subjected even on a minutest level of lived life to the codes of class, or caste, or gender, either separately or cumulatively or in different combinations. This exploitative practice could be—seen taking place in a myriad ways on a whole range of visible to invisible patterns and states of violence.

The post-modernist kind of 'specificity' only succeeds in isolating these micro-forms of exploitative practice as reified metaphysical entities subjectively perceived by the individuals in separation. And all those metaphysical entities hold out or assume many shapes of fear, anxieties, and threats under which the humans labour.

This is an account of the ontological condition of the so-called 'mainstream' civilization in Mahasweta's stories in *Imaginary Maps*, which imposes itself on the tribals in India.

The tribals in India, like all other indigenous peoples in the world, have inherited a pre-feudal value-system which did not suffer alienation of man from nature and hierarchization. Sobors, the haunting tribes, Mahasweta says :

> ....will beg forgiveness if they are forced to fell a tree; you are our friend. I do this because my wife doesn't have any food, my son doesn't have any food, my daughter starves. Before they killed an animal, they used to pray to the animal : the bird, the fish, the deer. (ii)

"Residual" (Raymond Williams : 3-10) in character, the tribals in various parts of India have no sense of property and no notion of money. There is no dowry system. Widow remarriage has always been the custom among the Austric and Dravidian tribes of India. And rape was unknown to them. That is to say, they are not as yet totally caught in the web of reified social relations like exchange-value. Their consciousness is determined not by a complex of metaphysical entities like reason constituting the social being of man in class/caste society. Instead, trust or intuitive belief in the fellow human beings forms the basis of their aboriginal social being nestling in the lap of unalienated nature. And so their social practices as human beings or human practices as social beings are still inexhaustible, although existing spiritually outside of the ethos of the dominant mainstream civilization or culture. Hemmed in by the latter all around physically, the tribals do not understand the "mainstream machinations" (iii) but feel threatened.

Yet the absence of violence-packed social relation among them renders them ineffective and incapable of resistance and makes them acquiesce in their lot when the forest land cleared by them is forcibly taken away from or when in recent times the inalienable right over their land is made a mockery of by the benami transactions of the mainstream.

The bonded labour system which was introduced by the British to placate a new class of feudals for their own benefit was officially abolished by the Government of India in 1976 itself. But the vulnerability of the tribals is such that "the bonded labour system, in its naked savagery and its bloody exploitation of woman" (iv) still flourishes in backward feudally oppressed districts in Bihar and other parts of India. And what is more, "decolonization of India" (iv) has done greater damage to them. The tribals whose civilization is built on the basis of ethical singularity (xix) which bears no alienation from "Nature, the sacred of other of the human community" (203) and so brooks no violence-packed dichotomous relation, became an easy prey to the neo-colonials who knew the tribal ways inside-out. And the tribals who cherished their "archaic freedom" (120) looked for it in the past. This rendered the condition of their life into an ontologically vulnerable one with no stock in the present moment.

Thus, both the ontologies—of the mainstream society as well as of tribals—are rooted in their own logocentric universes of metaphysics of presence as being, out of bounds of history. This explains or clarifies the hiatus perceived in Mahasweta's statement in these terms. The mainstream society, *i.e.*, the establishment, to use the customary political jargon, have never really intended to help the tribals to change their life pattern because it is both unwilling and incapable to do so. And the tribals, we have Mahasweta's word for it, "...have always wanted to change their life pattern." (viii); but not on the terms of the mainstream incorporating the imperialist exploitative ethic. None-the-less, the tribals are at a receiving end and the powers-that-be do not and cannot help them. And so, instead of submitting their self-respect or dignity, they cling on to their archaic or ancient freedom—the freedom of their ancestors. Thus, both tribals and mainstream are trapped, not in 'history' but in an a-historical situation of ontological parity.

But the realist-activist fiction as 'imagined history' by Mahasweta is not merely a narrative which visages an *aporia* of deconstruction in the condition of the tribals. The inhumanity of the metaphysical a-historicity is continually interrogated in her fictional narratives by the lived human life. It calls for the need or a possibility of action to change. This need or possibility is suggested by the characters and their actions in situations where the inexhaustible human spirit is pitted against the oppressive ontological social reality.

The characters modelled on real life heroes or heroines by Mahasweta in *Imaginary Maps* testify to this fact, as they grope towards becoming 'organic intellectuals'. They are an instance of "the celebration of the organic intellectual in Mahasweta's work and writing-work" (xxiii), to borrow the words of Gayatri Spivak. In the words of Gayatri Spivak again,

> When the subaltern 'speaks' in order to be heard and gets into the structure of responsible (responding and being responded to) resistance, he or she is or is on the way to becoming an organic intellectual (xxi).

Originally, "organic intellectual" is a Gramscian idea which is borrowed by Spivak. It is tailored to suit the description of those individuals who have the benefit of exposure to mainstream values like education. This is so, in the case of the tribals themselves. But at the same time, there are others coming from the mainstream, who through conscientization and politicization "through left struggle" (xxiii) work for the uplift of the oppressed tribals. Mahasweta Devi herself is an example of this kind. These intellectuals can communicate with the tribals only on a level of "ethical singularity" (xix) only if they cast off the ossified metaphysical value-system through commitment to action to bring about change. 'Ethical singularity' is defined by Spivak as reciprocal response involving "responsibility and accountability" (xix) and eagerness to exchange intuitive kind of "Love" (203), which is the mode of expression or behaviour of the tribal (who is not subjected to the process of 'othering', through alienation). Unless an organic intellectual functions on the level of ethical responsibility among the tribals, he or she cannot effect "a large-scale mind change" (201) in them—a change of 'mind' atrophied by the age-old oppression—for collective action. In this endeavor 'reason' which stands for the oppressor has obviously no place.

It is possible, in fact, desirable that organic intellectuals emerge from among the tribals for any real change to take place. But owing to the inhumanity of the ontologically-given oppression by the mainstream as well as on account of the 'mind' or the atrophied self of tile tribals, this possibility is continually negated as could be seen in the stories under the title *Imaginary Maps*.

The textualization of the impossible situation of parallelism of two oppressive ontological states of mind and the consequent conditions of existence cited in the beginning of this essay, is in fact interrogated by the three stories by Mahasweta. The plots and action of the stories are as faithful as could ever be to the situations in real life. They are instances of lived life—acts of suffering and resistance—that is, undying human practice. There is obviously an intended emphasis on the 'organic intellectual' acts of the characters which drive home the point of possibility of resistance (which is basic to change), mostly passive though, except in the case of Mary Oraon in "The Hunt".

Mary Oraon is an "eighteen year old tall, flat featured, light copper skin" (2) girl, was born of Bikhni, a tribal mother and an Australian father. The son of one Mr. Dixon the ex-colonialist landlord who owned before Independence a timber plantation and a bungalow in Kuruda village near Tohri, a coal-halt for the train, came back in 1959 to sell away the bungalow, the forest and everything else. "He put Mary in Bikhni's womb before he left" (2). Bikhni who worked as a servant in the house of Dixon gave up Christianity to be employed by Prasadji from Ranchi who bought the bungalow. Thus without her knowledge, Bikhni's life has been dictated to and imposed upon by the transfer of power from the imperialists to the native epigoni of imperialism—from colonial to post-colonial masters.

The child was Christened by the local Priest as Mary Oraon who grew up to pasture the Prasads' cattle and sell custard apple and guava from the Prasads' orchards in the Tohri market. She takes the train to Tohri with vegetables from the field. She is a hard and terrific bargainer with the buyers. She passes from the silence of Kuruda village to the bustle of the market in Tohri and back with equal ease. She has her "share of imperialist blood" (xxiii) as well as 'ethical singularity'. In other words, she possess "a transvestism of spirit" (xviii). Thus Mary Oraon is an instance of the "traffic of same-and-othering" (xviii); that is, *differance*, to use deconstructive jargon. Being a tribal and woman she is also a gendered other member of the metaphysical dichotomy. But at the same time, there is the alien essence of reason she has inherited in the circumstance of her birth. In tune with nature, the sacred other of woman in indigenous tradition, Mary Oraon zealously protects her honour in the face of the violence-packed dichotomous relation operating all around her. She spurns all attempts on her independence, keeps the savings she earns by picking the seed from the four mahua trees on the Prasad property as she is aware of the legal provision that "the right to the fruit goes to the picker." (3) She has chosen as her mate a Muslim youth, a leader of the marketers and a sharp lad. They will marry when between them they save a hundred rupees. But the distrust she has been a heir to makes her trust not even Jalim fully. Jalim and Mary exchange presents; but Mary will wear the saris given by him only after the wedding. Despite her share of alien blood and colour, she is accepted in the village society and her marriage with the Muslim boy is agreed to; Mary is thus both an insider and outsider to the tribal society of Kuruda. Although she is accepted, she is also feared by every one, especially the youth at the market who have designs on her. Yet, the trouble starts when Tehsildar Singh, the timber contractor descends on the peacefulness of the village. The sal trees planted by Dixon on fifty acres of the land attached to the bungalow have grown immense and ready for felling. The enterprising son of Prasad, Banwari, has entered into a deal with Tehsildar Singh and sold the trees to the latter with a profit for himself. The contractor thinks along with the trees and the cheap labour of the tribals he has claim to their honour also. He begins to make advances to Mary from the very moment he catches sight of her in Prasadji's bungalow where he is invited to tea. Being rebutted by Mary a few times, he has grown more insistent and offers a nylon sari to her through the Prasads. She takes it only to throw it at Tehsildar Singh in his tent when he is paying the labour their wages, with the words : "You think I'm a city whore? You want to grab me with a sari? If you bother me again I'll cut off your nose" (10). Yet the contractor's pursuit becomes even more singleminded, dogged and vicious. One day he even catches hold of her hand.

At first, Mary is scared and has lost her machete in the struggle. To her he looked the very animal. In order to ward him off for the moment she uses her guile of reason and the ruse of the gendered subaltern by telling him that she is "unclean" (13) that day. She fixes an appointment with him on the day of the feast, *Jani Parab* and asks him to wait for her behind a rock. Mary Oraon knows that the festival day on which a ritual of the hunt has been played by the tribals "for a thousand million moons" (12) is exclusively played by women every thirteenth year. It is called *Jani Parab* (the law of the forest).

On the day of *Jani Parab*, Mary wears a new, coloured sari and a red blouse gifted by Jalim and looked like "the flamboyant tree in motion" (15) representing symbolically a unique merging of 'the same and the other' overcoming for once the power of the metaphysical dichotomy. As she walked on her mission she is all aflame with a desire to hunt, "the big beast : A man, Tehsildar" (15). All the men in the village retired to an abandoned bungalow with the liquor bribed by Tehsildar.

Once she is with the animal, which traditionally ravaged the forest, behind the steep rock overgrown with the 'gilginda creeper' which concealed the bottomless ravine, she becomes more than equal to him in violence. The lopsided status of metaphysical dichotomy is reversed gradually in her as Mary drowns her own tribal inheritance of ethical singularity in liquor. She becomes an animal herself in spirit. She lifts her machete and strikes her game several times. The roles of the hunter and the hunted are thus reversed setting off symbolically negation of negation.

But the point is that this negation of negation is not only momentary but is subjective and individualistic, easily absorbed into the ontology of existence soon after the event. Mary Oraon's 'reason' does not extend beyond her love for Jalim and Jalim's as well as her safety in the midst of mainstream society all around. So, she escapes with the purse of Tehsildar Singh to Jalim in order to escape with Jalim to "somewhere" (16), where the law of the mainstream does not track her down. In this sense Mary does not measure up fully to the idea of 'organic intellectual', although "in her case, a share of imperialist blood and her consequent singularity are emphasized" (xxiii), as Gayatri Spivak thinks. Despite the transvestism of spirit in her, the essence of reason present in her does not operate on a collective level for it to build a structure of resistance, her act of revenge does not bear "the public use of Reason" (205) of Enlightenment which in a moment of supplementation with the "silent gift of the subaltern" (205) may make one an organic intellectual in the real sense; an organic intellectual, for whom history consists in change.

The exploitative metaphysical dichotomy in its crudest precapital form is demonstrated in the second story, "Douloti the Beautiful". The British-introduced system of bounded labour, variously known as *kamiya, seokia*, or *beth-begar*, has made the post-colonial bond-lord a government by himself. He became so "by lending money/And we [the kamiyas] have become kamiyas/we will never be free" (21).

Ganori Nagesia, before he became crook Nagesia, borrowed three hundred rupees from Munabar Singh Chandela who "keeps Dusad, Ghasi, Nagesia, Munda, Lohar, Oraon, Bhyian, Chamar, Parhaia as kamiya" 20—all tribals. He lives in the village of Seora. He has his son, an important government servant, living in the big house he built "on the bus route, in the market area, with an extensive garden" (20). Crook Nagesia needed the money because he was arrested along with some other tribals on the charges of stealing water-buffaloes from the market, and went to jail. On return, as was the custom he had to feed the community. "This is such a rule that you can't get around it" (21)—a hoary rule called tradition from the past of the tribals constituting the ontological condition of their existence. He also had to feast the tribals, for his eldest daughter and son were also married at the time. He had to give a goat to his son-in-law. And his family had to eat the flour, drink water and survive. And "Ganori became a kamiya when he took that money" (21).

To become a kamiya is, for the tribal, a "fate's decree" (21); but the brute power and the systemic violence are not discounted, though. The legend goes that :

> When a Nagesia child is six days old, that day our lord Fate will lower from the sky a yellow-turmeric-dyed string. For Fate will come down to earth on that string. He will look like a head-shaved brahman. (22)

He will not enter the room with the Nagesia mother and child. But with a thick pen he will write in high-Hindi in the cloth-bound ledger : "You will spend your life as you are born. You will never build a home better than a shanty" (22).

One Bono Nagesia who did not heed this traditional wisdom learns a fitting lesson. Bono was engaged by an agent for a coal miner at Dhanbad and came upon some money there in strange circumstances when he unintentionally killed a hooligan. Bono came back to Seora to build a house thinking in his artless simplicity that the bond-lord may take away pots and pans but not a house. He even sought the permission of the lord, Munabar, to build the house. But after Bono has build the house, Munabar's men locked up Bono in a room and set fire to the house. Then he was forcibly made to put his thumb print on a sheet of white paper in receipt of twenty-five rupees and declared a bond-slave hereafter. However, Bono decides not "to slave for his bond" (29) to repay the loan which acquires metaphysically endless proportions, by the unending labour of his body and the bodies of his wife, the sons and the daughters. Therefore, he decides not to perform the marriage of his son, Dhano, with the daughter of Crook Nagesia. He disappears from Seora, later to become a wandering ministerial in the service of a reformist journalist missionary, Father Bomfuller.

Meanwhile many things take place in the village. Munabar's white horse is dead when the lightning-struck tree falls over it. The 1961 census takes place. The tribals cannot understand why the enumerators refuse to write the names of the children who are dead. "Dead or alive they are my children" (31), a tribal thinks. The 1962 elections also took place. The tribals have no choice. They have to vote for the man as Munabar dictates. An educated Sadhu comes to the village to preach that they must worship the Mother Cow and unite to protect Hinduism. And on Ganori Nagesia's shoulder the axle of the carriage is put by the bond-lord because the latter's young ox which pulled the cart was eaten up by the tiger in the forest, on account of Ganori's carelessness. While trying to pull the cart, Ganori Nagesia falls on his face with the axle plunging into his back. After this Ganori Nagesia spends three months in Tehri hospital. When he comes out with his body broken and misshapen, he comes out as Crook Nagesia who is no longer equal to the bonded debt he owes to Munabar.

Crook Nagesia finds that a stage is set wherein no longer useful to his master, he is freed from bondage to Munabar by one Paramananda Misra, a relative of the local priest, only to take over Douloti, the younger daughter of Crook Nagesia. Ostensibly, he offers to marry her; but in fact he takes her in place of Crook Nagesia. Crook Nagesia is too ineffectual to resist in the face of the local conspiracy between the Rajput bond-lord and the brahmin 'god'. It is a hegemonic nexus of power of politics and caste or religion—a coercive force of metaphysical proportions over which the tribals have no power to exercise or resist. It is the post-colonial moment in the a-historical history of the world of tribals when the abstract privilege, greed and violence of the mainstream society could go to any lengths in perpetrating inhuman practices on the oppressed. The new-found bond-slave who is barely thirteen-years old, now, is thrown by her master as a piece of meat in the flesh market of the market-town of Madhpura. She is thrown as the live sexual quarry to a pitiless animal, Latiaji, a typical post-colonial aphrodisiac-consuming elite of a contractor who appropriates more than his money's worth of sensual pleasure from the body of Douloti.

Douloti is no gendered passive feminine but an innocent tribal girl who has become one of Paramananda's *Kamiya*. In her own simple innocent and human ingenuity, she understands the inescapability of her father becoming a Kamiya "as natural" (62) (in the sense of 'ontological').

"The social system that makes Crook Nagesia a Kamiya is made by men. Therefore, do Douloti, Somni, Raoti, have to quench the hunger of male flesh. Otherwise, Paramananda does not get money" (62). This simple logic of Douloti flows from her uncomplaining and undaunted acceptance, not acquiescence in, of the oppressive reality. She is too full of human spirit which refuses to be beaten flat and so "has taken the yoke of the Crook's bond-slavery on her shoulders" (73). She is highly skeptical of the statistical exertions of the missionary, Bomfuller, and his associates who count the number of the bond-slaves in the area in order to pressurize the government to prevent the practice. She has correctly sized up the problem to be too 'natural' to brook of statistics and any attempts at escaping.

When compared to Bono who tried in vain to escape the bond-slavery and is still escaping for the rest of his life trying to assist Bomfuller in his statistical work, Douloti, on the other hand, confronts it bravely and with ethical responsibility of love for her father.

In the end, "Having been bonded herself with three hundred rupees in 1962" (85) she has earned for her master more than forty thousand rupees. She develops fever and red swelling all over the private parts with burning sensation in the passage, when she goes to the hospital. Robbed and rejected at the Tehri hospital, she decides to go to her birth-place, Seora. Even before she reaches Seora, she is unable to walk any longer, vomits blood and falls "spread eagled" (94) across the map of India drawn outside the Basic Primary School in Bira village of Tohri block. She is discovered by the people of the village and the school-teacher, Mohan Srivastava who was preparing to hoist the national flag on the Independence day of India.

When she went to see the doctor at Tohri, he was surprised that "the human smile on the face of the unknown skeleton (of Douloti) had the innocence of a field of grain" (92). Thus the heroic and innocent Douloti who is yet to be drawn into the ambit of metaphysical 'reason' assumes a symbolic significance-representing the condition of post-colonial India. The kind of 'resistance' she offers against the oppressive reality and inequity is one of defiance of human spirit, instead of "internalized gendering perceived as ethical choice" (xxiv), as Gayatri Spivak thinks.

The third story, "Pterodactyl, Puran Sahay and Pirtha", presents yet another picture of the tribal resistance to the onslaught of modernist development. Mahasweta states in unequivocal terms that "*Pterodactyl* is an abstract of my entire tribal experience" (xiv). And that the Nagesia experience she has 'imagined into fiction' also represents the tribal experience all over India. This makes the three stories all of a piece in depicting the essence which is also "the agony of the tribals" (xiv).

It is an eye-witness, mind-seeing narrative of a journalist, Puran Sahay, rearing to go for a "sense of achievement" (97) in investigative journalism. He is invited by an old friend, Harisharan, the Block Development Officer of Pirtha Block, the tribal area in Madhya Pradesh: "Come, take a look, the State Government says 'No Story,' but here's Surajpratap's report, come to follow it up" (98). The problem is : for a long time the tribals have been dying in Pirtha. But the government is unwilling to declare Pirtha a famine area. The report submitted by Surajpratap earlier on has not seen light of the day. Puran too finds that in Pirtha the journalist is the most unwelcome thing for the government officials as well as for tribals though for different reasons.

The cartographic picture of Pirtha Block looks like some extinct animal of Gondwana land, a pre-historic creature which had fallen on its face. Full of hills with undulating terrain and narrow passes, the area is difficult to negotiate even with trucks. In rainy season, Pirtha has plenty of water flowing down the hill sides and drought in summer. A canal which has proposed to be built as part of Madhopura Irrigation scheme joining the Pirtha river would have solved the water problem for the people of Pirtha. But the scheme did never get started, although with great pomp and circumstance the inauguration ceremony by a minister was performed eleven years ago, according to the Sub-Division Officer. The area has been grossly neglected; although there has been no lack in developmental funds which are hijacked by the rich contractors and corrupt bureaucracy.

The state government did not want Pirtha to be in the news because already its honour suffered a set back on account of the Bhopal gas incident. It did not start a health centre in Pirtha; instead, the people dying of enteric fever are brought into town. The SDO who has reported this to Puran says that the fever "started from the polluted water supply" (99); but he does not know the cause for pollution. "We sent water...the water *tank* didn't get there. Both the *truck* and the *tank* had disappeared", he added, "I myself had posted guards at the polluted wells. The tribals then beat up guard, drank the water, and then : epidemic" (99).

Later in the day, Puran knows the cause for the pollution of water from his friend, B.D.O. : "a bit of rain in the middle of the drought" (122), ironically. But in hard reality, it is a fall-out of the development as a statistical matter *sans* humanity. It is as though the fate of the tribals is predetermined, by the system around them. In the absence of the B.D.O., Harisharan, suddenly, the 'Farm Aid Week' was declared and the workers came and sprayed insecticide all over the dusty fields" (122) parched up and dried in drought, on which the tribals could not grow 'Kodo-Kulki crops'. They did so to spite the BDO who tried to prevent the fraud in fertilizers practiced on the tribals by the men of his department in connivance with the traders. And when it rained the poisonous water from the fields flowed into the wells they dug; the rings for which were provided by the B.D.O. himself.

The tribals began to dic by drinking that water and by eating the kajra root, their chief hope in drought, which absorbed that water. But even if they die, you don't know it until the patient gets to the hospital centre (123) situated at Bhalpura. By the time the B.D.O. Harisharan returned already five girls, young women, and children had been brought by the waiting jackals from the plains "for a few sacks of the grain of the kodo" (123) and taken away on the truck. It is a fact several studies have registered that the roads that are built in the tribal areas have only helped" the owners of bonded labour, the money-lender, the touts and pimps, the abductors, and the bestial alcoholic young men lusting after tribal women" (109). And the road to Pirtha as part of 'development' takes away their 'archaic freedom' and enslaves them. To keep the process going, "In India, famine is being brought and sold by 'to whom it may concern" (125). The government does not recognize it as famine, only drought.

On entering Gabahi, the tribal village, Puran finds several harsh facts. As he was informed earlier and had seen the photographs taken by Surajprakash but suppressed by the administration, he finds an emaciated boy sitting on the stoop of a hut, who has engraved on the stone base of the hut the picture of a "being whose wings are webbed like a bats, body like a gigantic iguana, four clawed feet, no teeth in the yawning terrible mouth" (128). For the boy, Bikhia, who has become mute after engraving the picture, it is "the unquiet soul of the ancestors" (128). There is a close similarity between the shape of the carven prehistoric animal and the cartographic picture of the Pirtha Block. Shankar, the only literate tribal who lends a helping hand to Harisharan in his attempt to provide relief to the starving tribals, tells Puran that it is no use taking the enteric patients to the hospital because they have a death-wish cast on them by the roving shadow of the beast whose picture is drawn by Bikhia, pterodactyl. "The government does not want that we live. That's why they don't give us any help. The forefathers have been insulted, we could not protect their dignity. Now our life and death are not in our hands" (129-130).

This is as plain a statement as can explain untheoretically the abstract oppressive reality of lop-sided metaphysical dichotomy in operation and the ontology of the oppressor meeting with no other resistance than the ontology of assertion of archaic freedom of the ancestors; in which is proved the unequal but inexhaustible human practice. The paradigms of metaphysical reason do not hold good here. Only insights into the human action can be gained. Those insights may be judged obsolete by the ahistoricity of the history of metaphysics. But the historical realism of Mahasweta, I think, tells us a different story.

What the tribals are in need of at the moment is neither the fraudulent development, nor the scanty relief which could be provided by the individual government official like the B.D.O., but nature's bounty to wash away the poison and nourish khajra plants, which alone can assure them a life of dignity and self-respect. It is called rain, now.

Puran realizes that as long as he keeps his camera and tape-recorder, the tribals feel threatened in dignity and self-respect. He cannot win their trust. So he gives them away to Shankar, promising not to take pictures or tape anything, which is an act of respect for the ancient sole of the tribals.

During the night, after a sparse meal at the Sarpanche's, Puran is given shelter in the thatched room of Dahis who were the first to die of enteric fever. Attached to the house is a shrine into which Puran was warned not to enter. Bikhia was sleeping in front of the engraving. And Puran fell into deep sleep as soon as he lay down on a mat. That night it rained and into Puran's room "came the soul of the ancestors of Shankar's people" (141). Hearing the sound of breathing from the shrine, Puran mobilizes his numb body to get up and walk toward the shrine. Through a gap in the thatch that was blown away; the lightning flashes in the rain to make visible a dark form sitting on the floor. "From the other side of millions of years the soul of ancestors of Shankar's people looks at Puran, and the glance is so pre-historic that Puran's brain cells, spreading a hundred antennae, understand nothing of the glance" (141-42). On seeing it, Puran backs off carefully into the rain and sits on a stone resolving his mind not to say anything about it : "It wants refuge with Puran, Puran can not betray this, for any reason at all" (142). It is an encounter of trust—of ethical responsibility—

outside the ambit of reason between the archaic freedom of the tribal soul and Puran. Puran, as an organic intellectual, has dissociated himself —de-classed or decasted—from the essentialist spirit of his ancestors influencing his individual being. He recalls what Saraswati, thirty two, a school-teacher and who has been waiting patiently and with love since her eighteenth year defying her parents to marry Puran, once said on hearing the news of a sister of her friend being burnt to death by her husband over a dowry problem : "Ramachandra is the ideal of caste-Hindu men in Bihar. What did he not do? Political treachery, murdering the powerful by trickery, subjugating the powerless for political profit, burning his wife, deserting her when she is pregnant, killing the Shudra sage Shambuk—I don't think the high caste men of Bihar will ever be able to shake off Rama's influence" (142).

Shaking off that influence by Puran, has qualified him for this encounter of ethical singularity with the tribal soul. Puran now knows that he can save the dignity and self-respect of the tribals by choosing not to expose this reality to the newspapers and scientists, inviting invasion of the life of the 'starving' yet "living human element" (142) of the tribal life. Therefore, he decides not to do so. Now, Bikhia comes and holds his hand. He even puts his head on Puran's feet in gratefulness. Bikhia also has seen that ancestor lying on the floor in the shrine. Bikhia has received his ancestral soul. That is why his face is now so full of a quite wisdom. But what has Puran received? He put aside from his being the myth of Rama and received the love and respect of the tribals. When Shankar comes in the morning to take Puran away, he tells him, "You have brought this rain, the people of Pirtha are now in your debt" (144). The miracle they have been waiting for has happened—the miracle which "can bring good luck into this intolerable existence!" (145) of the tribals.

Later, Bikhia and Puran seek out a secret cave. As they walk on Bikhia seems to have become the ancestral soul. They go through a series of caves across the Pirtha river, follow a dark cavern which "goes down to the hill base" (177). Into this most secret and primal depths of darkness, they leave the hurt ancient beast of the tribal soul. This part of the story confuses the contours of reality, reason and fancy acquiring the characteristics of a post-modernist narrative.

It is after their return when Puran prepares to leave for the plains and bids good-bye to Bikhia, the latter speaks : "Yes Babu". He doesn't say come again but "come at the drought" (195). Apart from a jocular reference, there is also a suggestion that 'drought' has assumed for the tribals an ontological significance. As the rain-bringing miracle man, Puran, must come then. It is as though the civilized world and the tribals are engaged in a pitched battle, each ranged on a parallel line, never to meet but the one seeking to displace or root out the other. But as Shankar says :

> 'The ancestors soul let us know that all the places it visited are ours... (195).
>
> "They [the tribals] will not leave, they will not go anywhere leaving those stones, hills, caves and river..." (195).
>
> "If they [the civilized world or government] want to give us aid, let them give it to us here" (195).

The tribals refuse to be beaten flat. They are unwavering in their resolve to be treated on their own terms.

As the conscientious journalist Puran, who is qualified to become an organic intellectual knows that to build a communication-point to establish contact with the tribals" (196), one "must love beyond reason for a long time" (197). He has come to believe as he tells his friend, Harisharan :

> We [the civilized world] have lost some where as to Bikhia's people, to Pirtha. By comparison with the ancient civilization modern progress is much more barbaric at heart. We are defeated (196).

Mahasweta Devi arrives at this understanding obviously by deconstructing history and by resorting to a post-modernist kind of literary discourse (granting that Spivak's translation has not meddled with the original in Bengali). She introduces the myth of the pterodactyl, a creature of a-scientific and unmythological existence, but psychologically real in the tribal mind—as a decentering device to deconstruct history and denote the kind of space the tribals exclusively guard for themselves, which amounts to negation of negation.

WORKS CITED

Derrida, Jacques, "Structure, Sign and Play in the Discourse of the Human Sciences", *Contemporary Criticism : An Anthology*, ed. V.S. Sethuraman, Madras : Macmillan India Ltd., 1989.

Mahasweta Devi, "The Author in Conversation", *Imaginary Maps*, Calcutta : Thema, 1993.

All page references, hereafter are to this edition of the text and will appear in parenthesis at the end of quotations.

Spivak, Gayatri Chakravorty, "A Literary Representation of the Subaltern :

Mahasweta Devi's 'Stanadayini' ", *Subaltern Studies V : writings on South Asian History and Society*, ed. Ranjit Guha, Delhi : Oxford University Press, 1990.

See Blurb to Mahasweta Devi, *Imaginary Maps*, *op. cit.*

"Residual" in the sense Raymond Williams uses the word in Raymond Williams, "Base and Superstructure in Marxist Cultural Theory", *New Left Review*, 82 : December 1973.

8

Possible Stories and Multiple Endings : Rukun Advani's *Beethoven Among the Cows* as an Open-ended Narrative

DR. K. DAMODAR RAO
Department of English
Kakatiya University, Warangal

Rukun Advani's first novel, *Beethoven Among the Cows*,[1] is a free-wheeling, frolicking, multi-fibred roller-coaster of a narrative that makes wild, firm, and imaginative forays into the recesses of the self and the nation's history. Some of the parts of the narrative were earlier published as short stories and the episodic text offers a unified vision by projecting the linking line of coming-of-age of two brothers—the elder one being the narrator and the younger one focussed upon from and revealed through the narrator's standpoint—and also by striking a parallel between the individual and the political. The novel has been hailed as "Symphony in Purple Prose,"[2] as "a well-formed cerebral construct"[3] and "a most powerful novel on contemporary India."[4] In his review of the novel, Mukund Padmanabhan observes that the novel provides a kaleidoscopic pattern of growing up in India with all its tensions, fears, and complexes. He says :

> By weaving together dreams, history, fantasies and the everyday, Rukun Advani's *Beethoven Among the Cows* creates an illuminating and kaleidoscopic pattern that reflects the confusion and turmoil that attend growing up in post-Independence India. Written in a vein that is (quite astonishingly) at once ever playful and always serious, this ferociously intelligent novel grapples with questions of alienation, identity and belonging against a vast and chaotic backdrop that covers Nehru's death, the collapse of communism and the growth of communalism.[5]

According to Rukun Advani, the novel is presented within "a Nehruvian framework" as it "begins on 27 May 1964, the day of Nehru's death and ends after the demolition of the Babri Masjid with the symbolic end of Nehruvianism."[6]

Beethoven Among the Cows bears an unmistakable imprint of Salman Rushdie's *Midnight's Children*. The opening of the novel is an unabashed acknowledgement of Rushdie's influence. While Rushdie's novel takes Saleem Sinai's birth on the day of independence as the starting point of the subsequent dazzle of a drama, Advani's novel starts with the birth of the two brothers in the Nehruvian era. The invocation of Rushdie is but natural as Rukun Advani attempts to create an open-ended, self-reflexive narrative in the mould or Rushdie's novel. The opening lines of the novel read thus :

> At the midnight hour when clock hands joined palms in respectful namaste and India was born, my brother and I weren't even twinkles in our father's eye, perhaps not even specks in his pool of protoplasm. We arrived some time later, both on the afternoons of different years... (11).

Rushdie's no-holds-barred narrative, the classic of a Post-modernist text proved to be a path-breaker in Indian fiction in English. In a recent interview given after the release or his latest novel, *The Moor's Last Sigh*, Rushdie recalls the impact his first novel had created and says that it enabled "an enormous number of wonderfully gifted writers in English...to write their own work."[7] While "combining the elements of magic and fantasy, the grimmest realism, extravagant farce, multimirrored analogy and a potent symbolic structure"[8] Rushdie unleashed the amazing energy of the novel and in the process combined the "non-fiction novel and the far older political allegory."[9] What he aimed at and achieved was "not completion, not rounding off, but opening out."[10] True to the dynamics of the new novel, time-tested, worn out themes of war and peace, love and jealousy, crime and punishment were discarded by the experimentalists in preference for history and contemporaneity. In the words of Hasan Suroor, the new crop of novelists are engaged in "reworking old myths drawing on historical characters—or turning inwards portraying private griefs and dilemmas."[11]

Rukun Advani's *Beethoven Among the Cows* portrays such personal dilemmas, identity crises and also the country's chequered history marked by collapse of an otherwise workable system, destruction of potential in a new, independent India, gory exhibition of violence in public life and the brazen flaunting of religious card by power-greedy politicians. According to Sanjay Iyer, Rukun Advani's novel links "a personal history with a larger, episodic account of a nation's roller-coaster progress."[12] At the personal level, the two protagonists remain powerless and they retreat into a world of fantasy and music. Despite the occasional silverlinings, the history that cast its shadows on their persons has been grim, oppressive and suffocating. At the end of it when they wish to see the Taj and embark on their first journey to Agra, it was destined to end in disaster. The carcass of a cow on the railway track, communal riots in Agra and the closing down of the Taj for visitors only confirmed the fears of the narrator that the Taj would be the next target of the criminal-politician-fundamentalist conspirators. But the story does not evolve in a linear fashion; ideas, stray thoughts, passing references, allusions and incidents form leitmotifs which decide the structure and form of the novel. In Advani's own words, he was interested in creating an atmospheric universe rather than a solid, linear plot, structure and story :

> I think the book asserts that personal notion of a country which has to exist in large measure as a country of the mind, as an ideal, as fantasy.... I was more interested in the possibility that images and leitmotifs and patterns of thought can structure episodes into an atmospheric universe which is peculiar and distinctive, as opposed to fictions which give more place to plot and character. This really means according priority to the poetic quality of words and phrases and sentences rather than to their straightforwardly recognised meaningfulness.... It's what you find achieved most completely in Beethoven, Bergman and Dostoevsky.[13]

The narrator is often mystified as to how the two of them looked so unlike each other in physical features: His brother looked like Zeus in his youth and later like Beethoven while he was like a "higher rodent," at best "a rat" (78) and came closest to E.M. Forster (79). The narrator suspects that this could possibly be due to the fact that their mother breastfed his brother while he was denied the same : "He looked like Zeus and later Beethoven and was made of some special jelly which must have gone into him on account of our mother always letting herself into his mouth and denying me" (134). This, however, did not deter them from sharing their dreams, anxieties and fantasies. Their lifelong obsession was Beethoven's "Emperor" Concerto "in which the melodies seemed to give sufficient form to all the feelings" (98) they had ever harboured. It helped them "transform soulful torment into aesthetic torrent" (99) :

> There was an immense, impassioned, ordered turbulence about that music which set in perspective everything else in life and made it seem the highest cathartic interruption within the general desirability of silence (99).

As a unifying principle it runs through all the seemingly different stones of the narrative, and the composer's "Emperor" Concerto, in the words of Khushwant Singh, "only provides the background music."[14]

The cows that appear in the opening and closing pages of the novel are obviously intended to bring out the parallels/polarities between the personal and the communal with a carefully structured symbolic scheme. The first cow is an endearing one that frequented the house of the narrator being constantly fed by old issues of *The Hindu* and *Reader's Digest* by the narrator's father. The cow was called Mrs. Gupta because she resembled Mrs. Gayatri Gupta living next door : "They were both placid ruminants with spindly legs and they chewed just like each other, with the same muscular motion of their jowls" (12). The cow's digestive tract "transcended communism, culture, conflict ..." (15) and swallowed everything. It truly belonged to the Nehruvian era. The carcass of the cow on the railway track in the last pages of the novel that hinders the journey of the two brothers to Agra is a grim reminder of the tension-ridden, turbulent and troubled communal course the country has traversed. In between, in the process of the two brothers growing up into adolescence and adulthood, tragi-comic situations abound, suppressed urges come to the fore, question of identity brings along new crises, and the nation's history continues to cast dark shadows which are all described with comic irreverance. One such incident was the compromise made by the principal of the school in respect of the large photograph of Gandhi. It was the period when Gandhian idealism was being gradually replaced by more pragmatic outlook and business enterprise. As the narrator's school authorities make arrangements for the Martyrs' Day that year, they realize that the large portrait of Gandhi had gathered dust, cobwebs, and partly spoiled. The principal, "a retired Colonel of correct demeanour" ordered a replacement but the one arrived was a much smaller one. The excuse offered was that the company no longer did large Gandhis. They inform that large portraits of Nehru were available. The principal was a man of pragmatic approach and settled for a large Nehru instead. The following account is at once elegiac and playful :

> He recognised at once that ascetism and cheap cotton were things of the past and assented to the laws of the market. A

> diminished martyr came up at a lower height on one side of the hall, and pride of place was given to Gandhi's heir.... (20).

Nehru's death also comes as a shock to the generation fed on sparks of heroism, values of nationalism and virtues of unity in diversity. For the narrator who was a school-going child then, the news of the death of Nehru comes as an aberration as he was on the verge of getting his maiden century in a friendly cricket match. It was only later that he recognises the full import of the event :

> What could my mother, who had always seemed so invulnerable, possibly have felt to break down at the death of a man in the radio, a politician in the air? ... I simply forgot my own sorrow at the sight of her tears and realized that Nehru meant something deeper and far more emotional than an unfinished innings (32).

The second chapter, "Murder in May," brings out the pathos and bears ominous portents for future as nonchalance, outrage and cruelty become commoner sights which are a far cry from the dreams of visionaries. The people that gather around a bear lying in the street by the side of the bear-man are but samples of changing times. Only a hunchback-tailor whom the narrator affectionately called "Masterji"—and it stuck as it rhymed with his brother's "Masterji"—come forward to rescue the bear from the wrath of the public. But the crowd was already on the rampage and even the police target the bear to conceal their inability to control the mob. When a policeman shoots thrice at the bear's head, the narrator's horror could be described only in metaphors :

> Like John F. Kennedy in the distance to our west, like Vietnamese peasants in the distance to our east, like the flies which sat on our mangoes that morning, that bear never knew what hit him. He slumped down dead in a shaggy black heap over the body of his master. I saw the little dots of red blood that trickled out to mingle with the bear's black hair.... It was a native Indian dye, peculiar to our landscape, yielded by mixing casual brutality with the authority of uniforms and statistics. It was the colour of red-black gore on news print, a stain which spread out as one on the indelible colours of the country in my mind (69).

The adolescence of the brothers was marked by wild fantasies With his brother looking magnificent, the narrator could realize the fac that "future lay in wait only for his brother" (96). But his brother hac his own problems, strange urges to reach the unattainable. Looking a the picture of Elizabeth Taylor he would bemoan : "If suicide wasn't such a permanent thing...I'd commit it once a day. Some days maybe twice" (97). Watching the film, Cleopatra, both of them share the repressed sex-urges of the rest of the audience; but it was only for the sake of the two brothers that Elizabeth Taylor comes out of the screen to spend a few days with them. Mark Antony and Octavius Caesar, no longer antagonists, looked aghast at them : "For some reason, which I saw as their lack of vision, they couldn't see beyond the screen which separated them from us; their world lay in illusion" (104). In later years, they went native and adored Shabana Azmi to atone for their misguided youth. The illogic of their minds during this period was such that their wildest dreams came intensely alive "assuming shapes with a furious, unpredictable anarchy" (199).

The fifth chapter, "The Secret Life of Mikhail Gorbachev," funniest and most evocative, deals with the emotional breakdown of the narrator's brother—third such breakdown—by appropriating the image of Gorbachev as an arbiter elder-statesman and a repairer of souls even in personal relations but a compulsive loser on both political and personal fronts. Conversely and logically too, Raisa Gorbacheva is projected as a woman made of sterner stuff. Rukun Advani says that this part of the novel was written as a short story immediately after the collapse of the Berlin Wall that coincided with the breakdown of his marriage. He writes thus :

> It [the Berlin Wall] was a stable structure that became suddenly vulnerable and then apocalyptically crashed, like my marriage around the same time. So it seemed eccentrically logical for me to link political and emotional collapse by appropriating Gorbachev as a figure of fantasy.[15]

The narrator's god-like brother was "tall and handsome and wholesome and strong" (132) and looked full of foreboding. It brought the women towards him in flocks. But he also suffered from "short spells of intense sentimentality" (122). In fact, Raisa was his first love and the cause of his first emotional crisis. She used to call him affectionately "Jehova," since it fitted better with her own image of outward sternness. The narrator, through a long-distance call, requests Raisa to send in Gorby to rescue his brother from his emotional hook-up. The narrator knew that they were able to "disconnect" his brother from the tangle not merely because of their track-record but also because they were "distant, powerful, and cared about him" (134). Raisa had a reason to feel nostalgic about India because of her association with the narrator's brother while Gorbachev also feels attached to India because it was in Delhi's Lodhi Gardens that he chanced upon Raisa one winter morning. To Raisa's credit it must be said that when Gorby proposed to her, she did not know that they would become "king and queen" of Russia. Although they looked made for each other they differed in their temperaments :

> His strong sense of the bizarre made him irreverent and very good at rescuing lost souls. It seemed consistent with his own sense of the absurd that he, a man born never to rule, should have been driven by Raisa, once she'd acquired him in the Lodi Gardens, to assume in their later years an authority that he only wanted everyone to flout. By temperament he was a breaker of rules and she their maker (126).

For the narrator, Gorbachev was like Nehru who made "politics sound as though it had something to do with human beings" (137). He realizes that Gorbachev also needed a break from the emotional fatigue and the toll of falling walls as much as his brother and "organized one for them together" (138) by seeing them off to the hills.

If "The Secret Life of Mikhail Gorbachev" provides a hilarious account of the changing times, the next chapter, "S/He, or A Post-modern Chapter on Genre and Identity" is a biting satire on the noted theoretician, Gayatri Chakravarty Spivak who is referred to in the novel as Prof. Lavatri Alltheorie, a "post-modernist theoretician, boa deconstructor, discourse analyst, post-structural critic, feminist historian of subalternity, colonialism and gender" (145-46). The episode obliquely and overtly tears to pieces all that the Spivakan school stands for Rukun Advani makes it clear that he has but contempt for the school. He observes :

> My own hostility against this manner of writing is unambiguously prejudiced. This is because I am sceptical of the argument that historical and cultural studies require the levels of abstraction with which academics of the Spivakan school seal themselves off against straighter, more intelligible methods of expressing complexity.[16]

Whatever be the nature of the defence offered, one cannot help but concur with the view of Sanjay Iyer that the chapter is "a vicious, below-the belt dismissal of feminist theorists."[17] In the novel, Prof. Alltheorie is presented as a male who had changed his sex and became the champion of that gender. She created a jargon to which his brother and his associates always aspired. Her friends and admirers looked upto her as a model of excellence while her foes described her position with an equation of her past and present standing :

> Lavatri's Law : Incredible Articulation + Incredible Incomprehensibility = Incredible salary. By rumour she paid alimony to seven husbands and palimony to their seven predecessors. Socially she had the reputation of charming the pants off any man (147).

The narrator, now a private detective, is offered a job by Prof. Lavatri to enquire into the whereabouts of the person who wrote a damaging text to tarnish her image among the elite. The narrator succeeds in his mission by visiting the libraries of Indian universities and provides her with evidence of all his findings. This leads to a short but furious relation between the two. She had already shifted her base from "metroplis to periphery" ("US of A to India"), and her latest passion was to find her roots in Bengal by concentrating on Tagore and Bankim. This, the narrator's brother informs him, she wanted to do by being in the right gender, resorting to a reverse sex-change.

In "Incident by the Pangong Lake" the narrative moves back and forth in time as the narrator's brother occupies the centrestage. It focusses on the exploits of Vincente de Rozio, the childhood friend of the narrator's brother. He remained a hero in the imagination of the narrator's brother ever since he had thrashed their nagging tormentor-teacher whom they called "the Panther" and left school casually to evade punishment. The chapter also graphically notes the career and interests of Bhagwan Brahmani, a semen-collector and a manufacturer of test-tube babies based in Glasgow with whom the narrator's brother came into contact. Bhagwan Brahmani specialized in Third World sperm which was in great demand in the West. With the success of Sindhi enterprise in his genes, Brahmani bought and sold sperm by the gram that fetched a reasonable living. The narrator's brother got on well with all sorts of people, who never felt "to be guarded or defensive or closed up" (197) with him; Brahmani, for instance, showed his semen-bank full of phials to him. The description of the phials is a fitting commentary on the things in store for those Westerners with fast-changing tastes and needs :

> Brahmani's phials were mainly full of potential Hindus, Muslims, Buddhists, and Sikhs, but his collection was also known for its variety and elaborate subdivisions. He'd collected fluid from Hindu Jat, Haryanvi Sikhs, Bengali Muslims, Syrian Christian Keralites and Telugu Brahmins (197).

The narrator's brother also becomes a donor "to fulfil the needs of unknown women" (198).

The last chapter, "A Passage Through India," is about the near catastrophic visit—attempted visit—of the two brothers to the Taj, the "aesthetic centrepoint" of India. When the Golden Temple in Amritsar was stormed by security forces to flush out extremists, the fact dawned on the narrator that they had never been to Agra. He had a premonition that the Taj would be the next target of the power-hungry politicians, never wary of using the card of religion. He tells his brother : "You've studied history.... Nothing's permanent. I think we should go and see the Taj" (208-9). Looking at the picture of their parents, the narrator thinks that in the past, once their parents had planned a trip, they would not have hesitated a moment, gone ahead with their journey, and come back "secure, fulfilled, satisfied, all unease quelled" (211). It was not to be in the case of the two brothers. They postponed their visit to Agra unwittingly. The next time they thought of it with urgency was when "politics once again tore venomously into religion" and they were looking at another ruined monument, the Babri Masjid, which had stood "so harmlessly through the centuries that the people didn't know it was there" (212).

The trip to Agra turns out to be an "unsettling journey" (240) for the two brothers. A few kilometers away from Agra the train comes to a halt because of a carcass of a cow on the track. When they reach Agra in the early hours, they come to know that curfew was imposed in the town, that there were riots the previous night and the Taj was closed for visitors until further notice. Worse, as the two brothers try to make it to the house of their new-found acquaintance, Mrs. Sen, a stone comes hurtling down "reasonless" (237) through the air and hits his brother on the ear. Another stone hits the narrator on the head. Having been carefully nursed by Mrs. Sen, the narrator recovers and realizes that his own injury was light compared to the internal damage suffered by his brother. After the abortive trip, the narrator was sure of one thing : the Taj never called out to them as it once beckoned their parents (240).

Rukun Advani's narrative is marked by shifts of emphasis which are many-sided, multi-dimensional, thickly sparsed, and swiftly effected. As the narrative revels in the author's narration it also fretfully recognises the limitations of the processes of narration : There are too many things to be told and too many depths to be fathomed. All the same, it keeps a hectic pace and it goes on seemingly without end. While narrating the story of Vincente de Rozio and leaving it mid-way, the narrator expresses his preference for the unfinished, open-ended tale :

> What really happened to Vincente de Rozio after he ran away from the school seemed almost, in retrospect, a tiresome question. It was the sort of question asked by empiricist historians, or by people systematically conditioned to seek a banal satisfaction in the meaninglessness of ordinary events, never in the imaginative construction of possible stories and multiple endings that might prove more interesting, much more real, and infinitely more wonderful on account of their remoteness from the predictability of objective truths (194).

Even when the atmospheric creation is sought to be achieved, psychological states explored, and the impact of the personal and the social is sustained, it is conceived and executed with the skills of a maestro conducting a symphony. The description of the impact of Operation Bluestar and how it jolted the two brothers out of their slumber in worlds far removed from the country bears ample testimony to the multiple achievement :

> At that time he was travelling mentally through Scandinavia, listening to the music of Sibelius and watching the films of Ingmar Bergman. I was drifting soulfully through intergalactic time, reading Milan Kundera and formulating cross-cultural aphorisms....I was one with the cosmos. When I reached up I felt the womblike warmth of an Indian sky. Only the Buddha had fewer possessions and more salvation than I. Then, suddenly, the air got so thickly clouded with the bullets fired by politics into religion that my brother and I both went into a spin and had to bale out our solipsisms. We crashlanded back home with fractured minds (205-6).

Thus, Rukun Advani embarks on a maiden novelistic venture laden with seemingly chaotic, strikingly narcissistic, but refreshingly innovative stylistic devices.

NOTES

1. Rukun Advani, *Beethoven Among the Cows* (Delhi : Ravi Dayal, 1994). All further page references within parenthesis are to this edition.
2. Sanjay Iyer, "Symphony in Purple Prose," rev. of *Beethoven Among the Cows*, by Rukun Advani, *Indian Review of Books*, Oct.-Dec. 1994 : 29.
3. Mukund Padmanabhan, "Sparkling Wit," rev. of *Beethoven Among the Cows*, by Rukun Advani, *Indian Express "Expression"*, 3 July 1994 : 4.
4. Khushwant Singh, "With Malice Towards One and All," rev. of *Beethoven Among the Cows*, by Rukun Advani, *Deccan Chronicle*, 18 July 1994 : 8.

5. Padmanabhan, 4.
6. Rukun Advani, in conversation with Pankaj Mishra, *Indian Review of Books, Oct.-Dec.* 1994 : 28.
7. Salman Rushdie, interview, *India Today*, 30 Sep. 1995 : 101-2.
8. William Walsh, "India and the Novel," *The New Pelican Guide to English Literature* : *The Present*, ed. Boris Ford (Middlesex : Penguin Books, 1983), 258.
9. Ashutosh Banerjee, "Narrative Technique in *Midnight's Children*," *Three Contemporary Novelists*, ed. R.K. Dhawan (Delhi : Classical Publishing Co., 1985), 195.
10. E.M. Forster, *Aspects of the Novel* (Harmondsworth : Penguin Books, 1962), 170.
11. Hasan Suroor, "Race for the Booker," rev. of *Beethoven Among the Cows*, by Rukun Advani, *The Hindu*, 1 Oct. 1995 : xvii.
12. Iyer, 29.
13. Advani, *Indian Review of Books*, 29.
14. Singh, 8.
15. Advani, *Indian Review of Books*, 28.
16. Rukun Advani, "Academics as Writers," *Indian Review of Books*, Oct.- Dec. 1994 : 2.
17. Iyer, 29.

9

Centres and Margins : *Shame's* 'Other' Nation

DR. SYED MUJEEBUDDIN
Reader in English
Kakatiya University, Warangal

> The language of critique is effective...to the extent which it overcomes the grounds of opposition and opens up a space of 'translation' : a place of hybridity...neither the one nor the other...and changes, as it must, the very forms of our recognition of the moment of politics.
>
> Homi Bhabha[1]

Salman Rushdie's third novel, *Shame*[2], like its predecessor *MC*, again addresses itself to a centre other than the metropolitan one : authoritarian regimes that seek validity in doctrinaire Islam. If *MC* draws a stark, uncharitable picture of India, its parodic concerns, its subversion of the Indo-Anglian novel's conventions of national authenticity, even its severe indictment of the political leadership in India, are all yet marked by a frazzled hope. *Shame* on the other hand draws a bleak, harsh portrait of Pakistan.

Speaking about the contrast between *MC* and *Shame*, Rushdie has pointed out that the "moods" of the two books pertained to "a shift in my own mood": "I had the feeling, with Pakistan, of claustrophobia, and in India of wide open landscapes, and in simple terms the two books reflect those two views. The compass of *Shame* is more confined. *Shame* is not a portrait of a nation, it's a portrait of a ruling class, and *Midnight's Children* tries to be a bit broader than that...."[3] Thus India "if it means anything means plurality," while on the other hand Pakistan "although it has different races...feels more like a singularity, because

---

MC = *Midnight's Children.*

there is just the one religion and there's a much greater homogeneity both of language and faith, especially since the loss of the east and required a different treatment."[4] "The different treatment" that Rushdie metes out Pakistan results in its portrait as a desolate, despondent, oppressive and oppressing landscape. Bounded by a noose-like frontier that strangles its inhabitants, *Shame's* Pakistan is a dystopia, an absolute "area of darkness," that is incapable of generating ideas that liberate.

Unlike the "teeming," crowded, quality of the plurality of Indian life that Saleem in *MC* symbolises—the multitudes that jostle inside him and eventually break him up—*Shame* is riddled with images of empty, labyrinthine houses in remote places and frontiers surrounded by nothingness. Thus the house in 'Nishapur,' Omar Khayyam's "mother-country" is a "reclusive mansion" a "third world" that is "neither material nor spiritual" a "sweltering, entropical zone" where "nothing new seemed capable of growth," a "hideously indeterminate frontier universe," an "infertile and time-eroded labyrinth" and a "thing-infested jungle" (pp. 30-31), while Rani Harappa's house is located in the "backyard of the universe" (p. 94). Mohenjo, (Mohenjo-Daro means "the mound of the dead"[5]), the Harrappa country estate, is also a closed universe that stretches "from horizon to horizon," and is "afflicted by a chronic water shortage, (and) populated by laughing scornful monsters..." (p. 94). The house itself is described as a small labyrinth—"Verandahs run along all four walls; a long covered mosquito-netted walkway joins the kitchen bungalow,"—and is opulent—"And oil paintings and chandeliers and high ceilings and a flat tar-macadamed roof..." (p. 95). The frontier too is an empty place that sets off Omar's fear of the "Edge" and makes him a victim of vertigo forever afterwards. After *MC*'s crowdedness, the terrifying emptiness of *Shame's* landscape seems to symbolise a veritable trap, figured through the different kinds of solitary confinements that Iskander and Rani Harrappa experience. As Mary-Anne Paton rightly points out this emptiness and its accompanying solitude is Rushdie's image of hell—"one person miles away from another person."[6]

The narrative focusses on the "careers, corruptions, ribaldries and rivalries"[7] of its two main protagonists Iskander Harrappa and Raza Hyder, the former modelled on the personality of Zulfikhar Ali Bhutto and the latter on Gen. Zia Ul Haq, both powerful political figures in Pakistan until their violent deaths. In superb parody and burlesque Rushdie recreates the major strands of the contemporary history of Pakistan, and tells the story of a very small group of people who are "responsible for the *making of history* and for the controlling of power" and for whom "politics is a kind of family quarrel."[8] As Aijaz Ahmed points out this plot device is a brilliant "technical resolution" and successfully reflects "the monopolistic structure of dictatorial power and the very narrow social spectrum within which this power in Pakistan circulates."[9]

This centre of power is posited against the peripheral figures of the protagonist Omar Khayyam Shakil and the women, mainly Sufiya Zinobia the heroine of the novel who embodies in quite a literal way Pakistan itself. However there is another figure, the narrator himself, who emphasises his own marginal status and in aligning himself with the other peripheral figures of the novel[10] inaugurates an imaginative coalition between himself and them. In a passage couched in exquisite irony, the narrator conflates himself, his 'hero' Omar Khayyam Shakil, and the translatedly popular, 'Oriental' figure of Omar Khayyam, who the narrator points out in the text, was never very popular in his native Persia but existed in the West "in a translation that really is a complete reworking of his verses" (p. 29), very different both in spirit and content. "I too am a translated man," says the narrator, "I have been borne across. It is generally believed that something is always lost in translation; I cling to the notion—and use in evidence the success of Fitzgerald-Khayyam—that something can also be gained" (p. 29). Yet like Saleem in *MC,* the narrator being omnipresent, is also at the same time the centre of all things and makes claims of authority to speak about Pakistan. The narrator's articulation of Pakistan's calamity-ridden history is marked by an acute consciousness of his own intrusion into indigenous affairs and his virtual appropriation of the native voice as is evident in the defensive claims that the narrator makes to authority through an anticipation of the allegations of intrusiveness.

> *Outsider! Trespasser! You have no right to this subject*! ...I know nobody ever arrested me. Nor are they ever likely to. Poacher! Pirate! We reject your authority. *We know you, with your foreign language wrapped around you like a flag: speaking about us in your forked tongue, what can you tell but lies*? I reply with more questions : is history to be considered the property of the participants solely? In what courts are such claims staked, what boundary commissions map out the territories?
>
> Can only the dead speak? (p. 28)

The elliptical question hints at Rushdie's own awareness of the powerlessness of the peripheralised native and more importantly the chosen or enforced silence of the indigenous intellectual when confronted by the wrath of a totalitarian state : the imprisoned poet, who was hung upside-down by his ankles and beaten, "as if a new born baby whose lungs had to be coerced into action so that he could squeal" (p. 28). The image of an infant hanging upside-down also equates the 'voiceless' poet with Omar Khayyam Shakil who despite his name is devoid of any poetry and even a voice : "...you will note that my hero has already been ankle-hung, and that his name is the name of a famous poet; but no quatrains ever issued or will issue from his pen" (p. 28).

The poet's and Shakil's inability to "squeal" is Rushdie's cue to take up the mantle, "So here I am instead, inventing what never happened to me" (p. 28). Yet this "artistic journey," as Jean-Pierre Durix calls it,[11] is marked by an awareness that to produce a mythic Pakistan is to traverse the imaginative topography of Orientalist studies that produced and represented the East as the 'Other' and thus commit a further act of epistemic violence.

But he points out, as in the case of the Fitzgerald-Khayyam persona "something can also be gained" and offers the plurality manifest in his fabulous story of a fictional "Peccavistan." Thus what he actually posits against the monodic centre of Pakistan's singular discourse of religious and political power is the polyglot narrative of *Shame* itself:[12] parodies of holy texts,[13] ironic legends (the stories of Iskander Harrappa and Raza Hyder), cinematic motifs (movement back and forth in a mixture of flash-backs and montage), and a babel of voices that not only bespeak the narrator's own migrancy but also the marginal status of the women.

II

Rushdie's *Shame*, like its predecessor, *MC*, is again concerned with presenting an alternative view of history. If Saleem's 'authority' to speak in *MC* is derived from his being a sibling of the newly independent nation, the narrator in *Shame* conflates his migrant status with the status of Pakistan and his telling of its tale to the creation of the "*insufficiently imagined*" (p. 87) nation itself :

> When individuals come unstuck from their native land, they are called migrants. When nations do the same (Bangladesh), that act is called secession....
>
> I may be such a person. Pakistan may be such a country. (pp. 86-87)

Moreover, the term Pakistan itself is an acronym that was "born in exile which then went east, was borne-across or trans-lated, and imposed itself on history; a returning migrant, settling down on partitioned land, forming a palimpsest on the past" (p. 87). The narrator comments on how Pakistan was built : Pakistan is a "palimpsest" that "obscures what lies beneath," in order to build which, "it was necessary to cover up Indian history, to deny that Indian centuries lay just beneath the surface of Pakistani Standard Time. The past was rewritten; there was nothing else to be done" (p. 87).

The fact that the "job of rewriting history" was commandeered by the "immigrants, the *mohajirs"* (p. 87), implicitly lends the narrator, an immigrant himself, the authority to expropriate "the job of rewriting" that history once again. For, as he says, "I, too, like all migrants, am a fantasist" and

> build imaginary countries and try to impose them on the ones that exist. I, too, face the problem of history: what to retain, what to dump, how to hold on to what memory insists on relinquishing, how to deal with change...(pp. 87-88).

Yet unlike the making of Pakistan, the narrator's tale is one that insists on "excavating what lies beneath"[14]—the histories that Pakistan's intellectual and political leadership suppresses or excludes. If his "modern fairy tale" (p. 70) distorts the officially established truth it only does so in order to draw "better maps of reality."[15] Rushdie regards that the act of redescribing a world is itself a "political act" and a "necessary first step towards changing it," specially when the "State takes reality into its own hands, and sets about distorting it, altering the past to fit its present needs."[16] He sees politicians and writers as "natural rivals" for,

> (b)oth groups try to make the world in their own image; they fight for the same territory. And the novel is one way of denying the official, politicians' version of truth.[17]

Rushdie pits his truth against the "politicians' " version and his fabulous tale quite competently gives the lie to official truth. Rushdie's strategy is to blur the boundaries between fiction and truth, story and history. Rushdie himself has spoken about the need to see the connection between history and story in his work as an important one :

> ...I have always used a kind of historical method in the completely unmethodical way that is the luxury of fiction. I do think this connection of history and story important to remember. The Italian word *storia* means both things; the Urdu word *qissa* means a tale and it means history.[18]

Thus it is not surprising that the imposition of the fabulous "Peccavistan," with its sense of inequity, purity and conquest fused together,[19] over the 'actually existing' Pakistan, 'accurately' renders the socio-political life of Pakistan even as it records its 'exclusions':

> ...the issue of *Time* magazine (or was it *Newsweek*?) which never got into the country because it carried an article about President Ayub Khan's alleged Swiss bank account; or about the bandits on the trunk roads who are condemned for doing, as private enterprise, what the government does as public policy; or about genocide in Baluchistan; ...or about the attempt to declare the sari an obscene garment; or about the extra hangings—the first for twenty years—that were ordered purely to legitimise the execution of Mr. Zulfikar Ali Bhutto; or about why Bhutto's hangman has vanished into thin air...or about smuggling, the boom in heroin exports, military dictators, venal civilians, corrupt civil servants, bought judges, newspapers of whose stories the only thing that can confidently be said is that they are lies... (p. 70).

Shame revels in the paradox that its "military dictators, venal civilians, corrupt civil servants, bought judges," are pallid, phantom images of these 'exclusions,' caricatures of 'real' personalities. In positing the real with the fantastic and story with history Rushdie is actually presenting the reader with an 'anti-history': for unlike conventional histories that describe golden ages and glorious conquests, his tale about Pakistan is one where "clowns and goons play(ing) out the plots of high tragedies."[20] The novel is cluttered with 'great names,' and yet everyone of the characters bearing a great name shows his or her petty and paltry sides through his or her actions :[21] Haroun (named after the great caliph Haroun Rashid) is just a pretty boy and an insecure son of a great father; Babar Shakil (named after the founder of the Moghul dynasty in India) is a dissolute person who copulates with wooly sheep; Rani Harappa, very unlike her maiden name (Rani Humayun means Queen Humayun—Emperor Humayun was Babar's son, and father of Akbar, the great Moghul emperor) lacks authority even in her own house, where ayahs and old servants rule; Bilquis's father Mahmoud the Woman and his Empire Talkies ironically recall Mahmud of Ghazni (971-1030), known as the "Sword of Islam,"[22] one of the earliest Muslim conquerors of India and hence held among historians as one of the pioneers who established a Muslim presence and "Empire" in India; and last but not least Omar Khayyam Shakil, the peripheral hero with the great poet's name, very unlike the sense that his last name bears ("Shakil" means "well-formed," "comely" or "handsome"), is gross in his corpulence and intemperate in his habits and personifies shamelessness itself in the novel.

But above all *Shame's* 'anti-history' is about Raza Hyder and Iskander Harrappa. Again the names that Rushdie gives his protagonists serve his purpose of 'setting' them up. Thus in *Shame's* appellation for Gen. Zia Ul Haq, Raza Hyder, Rushdie deliberately uses the name Raza[23], to suggest the sense of the Hindi word for 'King,' "Raja,"[24] while borrowing the name Hyder itself from the name of the eighteenth century Muslim army commander from Mysore, Hyder Ali. Significantly, like Raza Hyder in *Shame,* Hyder Ali (1722-1782) started off from being a *naik*, a corporal, in the Raja of Mysore's army and "rose by ability to command the army."[25] However, he displaced the Prime Minister, and "retired" the Raja, making him "a prisoner in his own palace,"[26] to take effective control of the kingdom.

Yet unlike Hyder Ali's illustrious son Tippu Sultan (1749-53?), who became famous as the "Tiger of Mysore" and whose ability to strike terror in British hearts has attained folkloric status, Raza Hyder's progency, an idiot daughter, becomes a living testimony of his own shame and ultimately the cause of apocalyptic destruction.

Similarly, Zulfikar Ali Bhutto gets the Persianised name of Alexander the Great,[27] Iskander, while his surname Harappa is used to playfully suggest Iskander's lineage as dating to even before Alexander—the pre-historic Harappan civilisation itself. Both allegorical *personae*—Bhutto-Iskander and Haq-Raza—are grotesque caricatures of their great names, while at the same time being "pale shadows"[28] of their real-life counter-parts. What is significant, though, is that their 'anti-history' is presented as women's tales. The women who marched in from the peripheries to demand the inclusion of their "tragedies, histories and comedies" (p. 173) also get a chance to present their own version of the truth. The repertoire of "juicy-gory" gossip in Bariamma's house-hold underlines the strategy, again, of using 'story' to present a "sub-version" of history and forms the core of *Shame's* strategy. For as Rukmini Bhaya Nair puts it, in *Shame* narrative is "shaped as gossip" and is "creatively empowered to reclaim the metaphors of an elite history."[29] Thus if these gossipy tales are "the glue that held the clan together, binding the generations in webs of whispered secrets" (p. 76), it is through the repeated recounting, exemplified in Bilquis's story, that they acquire the sanctity of truth, of history :

Her story altered, at first, in the retellings, but finally it settled

> down, and after that nobody, neither teller nor listener, would tolerate any deviation from the hallowed sacred text. (p. 76)

Raza Hyder's remark to Bilquis after her 'initiation' marks this passage of story into history, "The recounting of histories is for us a rite of blood" (p. 77).

This telling of family tales, as pointed out earlier, actually constitutes creating an alternative, 'anti-history,' for unlike the epic heroisms and magnificent epochs that 'elite' histories speak of, these stories are,

> lurid affairs, featuring divorces, bankruptcies, droughts, cheating friends, child mortality, diseases of the breast, men cut down in their prime, failed hopes, lost beauty, women who grew obscenely fat, smuggling deals, opium-taking poets, pining virgins, curses, typhoid, bandits, homosexuality, sterility, frigidity, rape, the high price of food, gamblers, drunks, murders, suicides and God. (p. 76)

Bariamma's sardonic telling of Raza Hyder's tale, her story of the "strong-man of the nation," who is also a melodramatic "type who cried too easily" (p. 78), is one such example. The tale of the conquest of the "valley of tears" is delectably ironical :

> ... He returned a hero, having seized for our new holy land a mountain valley so high and inaccessible that even goats had difficulty in breathing up there; so intrepid he was, so tremendous, that all true patriots has to gasp—and you must not believe that propaganda which says that the enemy did not bother to defend the place... (p. 79).

This 'mock-hero' is further rendered pathetic when the tale of the birth of his "re-incarnated son" is told. In a deliciously wicked scene Rushdie and Bariamma poke fun at the General's refusal to accept "defeat" and his 'fighting' qualities, when his frenzied longing for a boy is shattered and Sufiya Zenobia, instead of the expected boy, is born. The terminology of the battle-ground used here, only sets off Raza Hyder's ludicrous attempt "to affect biology by a superhuman act of will" (p. 90).

> Defeat? But this was Old Razor Guts himself, conqueror of glaciers, vanquisher of frosty meadows and ice-fleeced mountain sheep! Was the future strong-man of the nation so easily crushed? Not a bit of it. Did the midwife's bombshell lead to unconditional surrender? Certainly not. Raza began to argue; and the words came in rushes, inexorable as tanks. The

> walls of the hospital shook and retreated; horses shied, unseating riders, on the nearby polo fields.
>
> ...
>
> And blasted from his lips like cannonballs : 'Genitalia! Can! Be! Obscured!' (p. 89)

This grotesquely comic tale, says the narrator, may have been "a little embellished during its many tellings and retellings," but he refuses to question "the veracity of oral tradition." (p. 90) Remarkably, the narrator's own tale complements and mirrors this "oral" tradition and if he too "embellishes" his story a little, it only serves to highlight the grotesqueness that lies hidden behind the normal and the perturbing corruption that official truth seeks to obscure.

The "pukka Peter sellers Indian" of Raza Hyder[30] is used to highlight the cruel, sadist ways of the General. The theatricality of his actions—praying on television and taking oaths on the Quran—actually set off his lies, so that his motto, "Stability in the name of God" (p. 249) is taken to be a joke, apparent in the Chief Martial Law Administrator's initials CMLA, which we are told, actually stand for *Cancel My Last Announcement.* The ruthlessness of the comic Raza is reflected in his readiness to murder his own daughter when he realises that she could be a danger to him.

The narrator similarly lampoons the democratic pretensions of the late Zulfikar Ali Bhutto through his fictional portrait of Iskander Harappa. Again like in Raza Hyder's case the severest indictment comes from the women's version of the truth—Rani Harappa's eighteen embroidered shawls that depict Iskander Harappa's 'anti-history.'

The embroidered shawls exemplify the ingenious, if tenous, intertextuality of Rushdie's conceits. For here, unlike Bariamma's 'folk-tale' of Raza Hyder's great conquests, Rani Harappa's shawls, as a motif, seem to be based on an actual source of history, albeit the history of England—the Bayeux Tapestry depicting William the Conqueror's conquest of England.[31]

Traditionally attributed to Queen Matilda, wife of William the Conqueror, and her hand-maidens,[32] the so-called "Tapestry," like Rani's "epitaph of wool" for Iskander (p. 191), "is in fact an embroidery in coloured wools on a linen base."[33] Rani's "eighteen shawls of memory" (p. 191) also bear similarity to the Bayeax Tapestry in so far as both testimonies are largely silent and pictorial, interspersed with captioned inscriptions and legends.

However, in the context of Rani's exilic condition and near-abandoned status, more important is the ironic evocation of a devoted Queen's proud tribute to her 'Lord and Master's' glorious conquest. For what is depicted in Rani's embroidered testimony is not the grandeur of a majestic personality but the 'truth' of Iskander's lust for power that masquerades as love for his people, and his insatiable pleasure-seeking ways hidden behind his "servant of Duty" (p. 192) facade. Appropriately given the title, "The Shamelessness of Iskander the Great" (p. 191), the embroidered shawls stand witness to everything that Arjumand, blinded by her love for her father, refuses to see—a saga of lust, revenge and terror, replete with blood and gore. Thus Rani's account of the 'life and times' of Iskander Harappa constitutes, unlike the Bayeaux Tapestry, an alternative version of official and elite history. It is a defiant act of subversion as well, for Rani not only sets the record straight but by signing her maiden-name, *Humayun,* she also seeks to retrieve her own self from "the mothballs of the past" (p. 191), and "the fine mist of oblivion" (p. 194) that Iskander had consigned her life into.

What is also significant about the embroidered shawls is the fact that they bear an inter-textual debt to Faiz Ahmed Faiz's famous *ghazal,* "Do Not Ask of Me, My Love"[34] a poem that Rushdie himself quotes in *SV* (pp. 334-35).[35] Though the poem's context is a different one, the startling conceit in the lines quotes below, demonstrates that *Shame* is acquainted with not only Faiz's ideas on elitist history but also the actual figuring of those ideas :

An-ginat sadyon ke tarik bahemana tilism
Resham o atlas o kamkhab men bunwa'e hu'e
Ja-ba-ja bikte hue kucha o bazar men jism
Khak men lithare hue, khun men nahlae hue
Jism nikale hu'e amraz ke tannuron se
Pip bahti hu'i galte hu'e nasuron se-[36]

In Victor Kiernan's translation these lines read :

The dark beastly spell of countless centuries,
Woven into silk and satin and brocade,—
Bodies sold everywhere in alley and market,
Smeared with dust, washed in blood,
Bodies that have emerged from the ovens of
diseases, Pus flowing from rotten ulcers—[37]

Elitist history woven as it is in "silk, satin, and brocade" hides the misery that countless people have suffered through times

> immemorial. If Faiz's unconventional juxtaposition of velvety luxuriousness with images of physical decay and corruption of the human body poignantly highlights the limitations of conventional history, Rani Harappa's shawls focus precisely on what is conveniently excluded in the recording of so-called great men's lives. Thus for each projected virtue of Iskander, Rani offers us an alternative view. Lasciviousness, egotism, revenge, torture, terror, election rigging, and death...the bodies sprawled across the shawl, the men without genitals, the sundered legs, the intestines in place of faces, the alien legion of the dead...*twenty, fifty, a hundred thousand dead, who knows, and not enough scarlet thread on earth to show the blood*, the people hanging upside down with dogs at their open guts, the people grinning lifelessly with bullet-holes for second mouths, the people united in the worm-feast of that shawl of flesh and death...(p. 195).

—everything about the "dark beastly spell" of Iskander's reign is woven into the brocade of Rani's shawls.

One notes that in Rani Harappa's shawls, Rushdie fuses together historical and literary motifs. *Shame's* metaphors and images—conceits, rather—function as palimpsests and signify a dynamic hybridity that is brazen and polemic in its politics, as against the "palimpsest" of Pakistan itself that expressly obscures "what lies beneath" (p. 87). Thus it is significant that in the palimpsest of the shawl, the West as history and the East as literature[38] are pressed into service to severely indict the corrupt power politics of ruling-class Pakistan.

If Rani Harappa's eighteen shawls constitute an "act of accusation on the grandest conceivable scale" (p. 193), the severest indictment of the insularity of Pakistani society is emblematised in Sufiya Zinobia. The puny idiot girl, "the wrong miracle," who blushed right from the moment she was born, is a personification of shame itself, her blushes signifying the shame of the world she is born into. A "saint" who endures the shamelessness of others (p. 141), Sufiya suffers until the latent violence, intrinsic to a marriage between shame and shamelessness (as *Shame's* logic goes) erupts and the mild, idiot girl becomes a ferocious, marauding beast. In the "bi-polar"[39] world of shame and shamelessness, the narrative of *Shame* suggests, the only solution lies in violence : "Between shame and shamelessness lies the axis upon which we turn; meteorological conditions at both these poles are of the most extreme, ferocious type. Shamelessness, shame : the roots of violence" (pp. 115-16).

Discussing this aspect of *Shame,* of the violence that Rushdie suggests is inherent in the dialectics of shame and shamelessness, Aijaz Ahmad observes that "violence is not in itself capable of regeneration, and it is doubtful, Fanon notwithstanding, that violence is intrinsically even a cleansing virtue." He thus finds the very dialectic—"of shame and shamelessness and their condensation in eruptions of violence"—governing the "conceptual framework of the novel" fundamentally flawed.[40]

Ahmad, in his otherwise astute assessment of *Shame*, here misperceives the violence in the novel as something that is there for its own sake—"violence...in itself"—and overlooks the fact that its *raison d'etre* is derived from its manifesto which is, as Peter Craven puts it, one of "political and historical action."[41] Thus if the novel itself, in its outspoken criticism and in its brutal satire of Pakistan's ruling class constitutes a political action, the narrator's attempts at retrieving the past that lies obscured beneath the palimpsest of the present reflects again an individual, even heroic action, much like the action that Saleem in *MC* takes in retrieving and 'chutnifying' his version of history."

However, more significant is the way that *Shame* shows its preference for women who are dynamic and aggressive and rejects the passive roles that women are reduced to playing and sometimes, under the pervasive influence of patriarchal values, even will this subjection upon themselves. Accordingly, almost all the 'normal' women in *Shame* are shown as passive or complicit with patriarchal values and are consequently rejected and are shown in the most negative light : thus Arjumand Harappa who is so blinded by her love for her father that she refuses to see even his most glaring omissions is condemned, like her mother to a life without love; the author's contempt for Naveed Hyder, and her propensity towards 'sitting on her hair,' is evident when he summarily dismisses the story of her rebellion as not worthy of comparison with Anna Muhammad's; Bilquis's disappointment in her own inability to produce a son marks her as complicit with patriarchal values; even Bariamma, embalmed in the fixity of her gossipy tales is subjected to the author's contempt and ridicule. It is only Rani and Omar Khayyam's three mothers, apart from Sufiya Zinobia that receive sympathy and understanding from the author.

Rushdie's thrust towards action is manifested in the name he gives his heroine—Sufiya Zinobia. Apart from the obvious reference to Sufism in 'Sufiya,' the name evokes the personalities of some of the women involved with the Prophet during his life-time. Thus in 'Sufiya' we also find the name of Safiyah, the Prophet's Jewish wife, and in Zinobia, the three women named Zainab integral in many ways to the Prophet's life—two of them his wives and one a daughter. However, more importantly 'Zenobia' is also the name of the third century Queen of Palmyra, famous for her "beauty and intelligence" and yet one whose "name has also been a symbol of ruthless arrogance."[42]

These revenant presences in the elaborate pun in Sufiya's name are indicative of the crucial point that Rushdie makes in the novel—of the beast that lurks in the beauty. Rushdie's use of the name is deliberately oxymoronic so that the pure and innocent but inactive and cloistered women of the Prophet's family are sharply contrasted with the ambitious and ruthless Zenobia.

This juxtaposition of the dynamic and the placid, the active and the passive in Sufiya Zinobia's name also becomes apparent in Rushdie's discussion of the other "ghosts" that "haunt" Sufiya's story : the British Pakistani girl, who was killed by her father because she had shamed him by making love to an English boy, the unnamed 'Asian' girl, who was beaten up on the underground by a gang of white teenaged boys, and the boy who had, impossibly, "ignited of his own accord" (p. 117) and burned himself to death. The narrator here delineates the predicament of people caught in situations where they are either the victims of other people's shame, as exemplified by the story of the Pakistani girl, or, are themselves mortified by their situations, as typified by the case of the unnamed girl. Reflecting on the latter's reluctance to talk about this incidence, the narrator points out that "it is a typical reaction, and the girl is not one girl but many" (p. 117).

The "burning" boy's case connects the humiliation suffered by coloured people in a metropolitan society with the sense of shame inflicted on women in "traditional" societies. The narrator ruminating on the televised images of racial riots in England, feels that the young people whose "shame burning on their brows" not only set "fire to the shops, police shields, cars" (p. 117) but also to the humiliation that they have suffered in a racist society :

> Humiliate people for long enough and a wildness bursts out of them. Afterwards, surveying the wreckage of their rage, they look bewildered, uncomprehending, young. Did we do such things? Us? But we are just ordinary kids, nice people, we didn't know we could...then, slowly, pride dawns on them, pride in their power, in having learned to hit back. (p. 117)

The narrator fantasizes a similar fury unleashed in the girl against the thugs who beat her up in the underground train :

> how she would have thrashed the white kids within an inch of their lives, breaking arms legs noses balls, without knowing whence the violence came, without seeing how she, so slight a figure, could command such awesome strength. ...I feel gleeful about this notion : it's a seductive, silky thing, this violence, yes it is. (p. 117)

The "seductive, silky...violence," however, as pointed out earlier is not a wanton phenomena. As the narrator points out, one has to find the energy and the fire in our own selves : "We are energy; we are fire; we are light" but what is important is "Finding the key, stepping through that truth...." In short, it is 'action' that engenders the "pride in...power" and leads to violence, which in its turn leads to change.

However, the fact that Sufiya Zinobia is the only one who can act renders Rushdie's perception of action problematic. Firstly the repeated "connections" that Rushdie makes while trying to show Sufiya Zinobia's plight as a universal predicament, robs her of the existential pathos that could render her action meaningful. Sufiya exists so much in the mind and fantasy of the narrator and the "ghosts" that he rigs up to contextualise her character, that the reader inevitably feels distanced from her. Secondly, the fact that the crucial act of "Finding the key, stepping through that truth..." occurs in the fantasy of the narrator and the madness of Sufiya Zinobia, turns the notion itself, of action, into an abstraction devoid of any pragmatic value.

Moreover, as Ahmad rightly points out, Rushdie constantly elides his political fable with a civil society "that is declared to be co-terminal with this state structure, equally deformed and irretrievably marked by its purported civilisation (Islam) and its generic origin (the partition)."[43] Also in emphasising action Rushdie exaggerates the role of individuals and ignores the role of constructive, group activism; as Inderpal Grewal points out the only time the organised effort of the women's movement in Pakistan is mentioned it is dismissed within the space of a paragraph.[44]

Nevertheless in *Shame* Rushdie has made a crucial move towards a consideration of social praxis as action and his next novel, despite its more controversial nature would have a maturer and more positive consideration of action.

NOTES

1. Bhabha quoted in Anne Maxwell's "Current Debates in Theories of Colonial Discourse", *Kunapipi,* Vol. 13, No. 3, p. 72.

   See also Homi Bhabha, "The Commitment of Theory," *New Formations,* 5, 1988, pp. 10-11.
2. Salman Rushdie, *Shame,* (1983) (London : Picador, 1984). All quotations are from this edition, with page numbers cited in parenthesis.
3. "Salman Rushdie," Interview conducted by David Brooks and Marie-Anne Paton, *Helix,* Vol. 19/20, 1984, pp. 64-65.
4. *Ibid.*, p. 65.
5. Timothy Brennan, *Salman Rushdie and the Third World : Myths of the Nation,* (London, Macmillan, 1989), p. 119.
6. *Helix,* p. 68.
7. Aijaz Ahmad, "Rushdie's *Shame* : Postmodernism, Migrancy and Representation of Women," *Economic and Political Weekly,* June 15, 1991, p. 1466.
8. Salman Rushdie, "Lecture/Interview," *Kunapipi,* Vol. 8, no. 1, 1985, p. 18.
9. Ahmad, "Rushdie's *Shame,*" p. 1466.
10. Whether this narrator figure is Rushdie himself is a moot point; however Aijaz Ahmad's insistence on viewing the narrator's voice as Rushdie's own cannot be dismissed easily especially since Rushdie himself has admitted as much.

    See (1) "A Dangerous Art Form," interview with Salman Rushdie in *Third World Book Review,* Vol. 1, no. 1. (2) "Lecture/Interview" in *Kunapipi,* p. 13. (3) The *Helix* interview, p. 58.
11. Jean-Pierre Durix, "The Artistic Journey in Salman Rushdie's Shame," *World Literature Written in English,* 1984 Spring, Vol. 23 no. 2, pp. 451-63.
12. Brennan points out that the many sub-plots of *MC* give way, in *Shame* to a mosaic of a chain of "juxtaposed and basically self-contained parables" so that the earlier novel's strong and "dominant" centre is replaced by several individual points of view. But Brennan here overlooks the narrator himself who is as central to *Shame's* narrative as Saleem was in *MC.*

    See Timothy Brennan, *Salman Rushdie and the Third World : Myths of the Nation,* pp. 122-23.
13. See Brennan's excellent "*Shame*'s Holy Book" in his *Salman Rushdie and the Third World : Myths of the Nation,* pp. 124-35.
14. Anuradha Dingwaney, "Authorizing Midnight's Children and Shame : Salman Rushdie's Constructions of Authority," Emmanuel S. Nelson, (ed.) *Reworlding : The Literature of the Indian Diaspora,* (Westport CT, Greenwood, 1992), p. 162.
15. Salman Rushdie, "Outside the Whale," *Imaginary Homelands : Essays and Criticism 1981-1991*, (London, Granta, 1991), p. 100.
16. Rushdie, "Imaginary Homelands," *Imaginary Homelands,* pp. 13-14.
17. *Ibid.*, p. 14.
18. Rushdie, *Helix,* p. 58.
19. *Peccavi,* "I have sinned," and Napier's famous coded telegraph, conveying his victory over Sind, jostles here with the meaning of the word "Pakistan," "the country of the pure."

20. Rushdie, "Lecture/Interview," p. 15.
21. Incidentally, a majority of these 'names' are traditionally associated with 'Indian' history, even though a large part of this history also happened in what is now Pakistan. It is worthwhile recording that not only has Pakistan been always a part of the Moghal empire, but also the traditional route for the Turko-Afghan marauders and Mongolian conquerors. Iskander's surname, Harappa, and the name of his country estate Mohenjo, are the names of the famous prehistoric sites, located in Pakistan but considered signs indicative of the earliest *Indian* civilisation. Rushdie is making sure that his readers wouldn't forget that "Indian centuries 1(ie) just beneath the surface of Pakistani Standard Time" (p. 87).
22. Stanley Wolpert, *A New History of India*, (New York : OUP, 1989), pp. 106-7.
23. "Raza" (Persian/Urdu) literally means "agree"; as a man's name it can mean one who agrees with the "will of God," or even the "will of God," itself.
24. See also Brennan, p. 120.
25. Percival Spear, *India : A Modern History,* (Ann Arbor : Michigan UP, 1961), p. 218.
26. *Encyclopedia Britannica,* Vol. 6, 15th edition, 1992.
27. A personality that finds mention even in the Quran—Zul Qurnain whose story is recounted in the chapter entitled *al-Kahf* (The Cave).

    See Abdullah Yusuf Ali, trans. *The Holy Quran,* (Beirut : Dar Al Arabia, 1968), pp. 760-65.
28. Rushdie, *Helix,* p. 59.
29. Rukmini Bhaya Nair, "Text and Pretext : History as Gossip in Rushdie's Novels," *Economic and Political Weekly*, 6 May 1989, p. 995.
30. Peter Craven, "Salman Rushdie's Rough Magic," *Scripsi,* Vol. 3, no. 2-3, 1985, p. 144.
31. Rushdie actually cites the landing of William the Conqueror and the Battle of Hastings in *SV*. Significantly, the immigrant-conquerors Chamcha and Farista, like William also "land" in Hastings.
32. *New Columbia Encyclopedia,* 4th edition, 1975.
33. Still popularly known as "la Tapisserie de la Reine Mathilde" in France, the Bayeax Tapestry is in fact now, correctly, attributed to Odo, Bishop of Bayeaux and William's brother who commissioned it. Interestingly though, like Rushdie's Pakistan which was born in the West and "which then went East" (p. 87) the Tapestry is regarded as being made in England, (more specifically, in St. Augustine's Abbey in Canterbury!), which was then taken to France.

    See R. Allen Brown, *The Norman Conquest,* "Documents of Medieval History Series," eds. G.W.S. Barrowa and Edward Miller, (London : Edward Arnold, 1984), pp. 172-73 and *New Columbia Encyclopedia,* 4th edition, 1975.
34. Victor Kiernan translates Faiz's *Mujh se Pehle si Mohabbat Mere Mahboob na Maang* as "Love, Do No Ask." See *Poems by Faiz,* Unesco, Vanguard Books, 1971, p. 65.
35. Rushdie in *SV* uses, what he calls a "variant" of Mahmood Jamal's translation of Faiz's poem. Neither does he quote the poem in full. The lines quotes here by me form the second stanza of Faiz's poem, which is incidentally also the part that Rushdie does *not* quote. (*See* "Acknowledgements" at the end of *SV*.)

36. The romanization (or transliteration) of Faiz's Urdu *ghazal* is borrowed from Victor Kiernan's book, *Poems from Faiz,* pp. 65-67. It has not been possible to reproduce Kiernan's usage of signs and symbols, and consequently his superb delienation of the nuances of Urdu, due to technical reasons.
37. Kiernan, *Poems by Faiz*, pp. 65-67.
38. Rushdie has often remarked that his work is read as "fantasy" in the West and as "history" in the East.

    See, for instance his interview in *Scripsi*, Vol. 3, no. 2-3, 1985, p. 113.
39. Rudolf Bader, "On Blood and Blushing : Bipolarity in Salman Rushie's Shame," *International Fiction Review*, 1988 Winter, Vol. 15, no. 1, pp. 30-33.
40. Ahmad, "Rushdie's *Shame,*" p. 1467.
41. Craven, "Rushdie's Rough Magic," p. 141.
42. *Columbia Encyclopedia* 1975.
43. Ahmad, "Rushdie's *Shame,* p. 1466.
44. Inderpal Grewal, "Salman Rushdie : Marginality, Women, and Shame," *Genders,* 1988 Nov., Vol. 3, p. 38 [pp. 24-42].

10

The Moor's Last Sigh : Creativity and Controversy

DR. PRADEEP TRIKHA
Department of English
Dayanand College, Ajmer

Salman Rushdie's sixth novel *The Moor's Last Sigh* (*The Moor's*) has upset lot of people. It has inflamed both enthusiasm as well as resistance of course not with the same intensity as his *The Satanic Verses* did. As one of the critics points out that the parallel between the two "....only brings out the old rivalry between reality managers and the outcasts from the programmed reality".[1] Both in *The Moor's* and *The Satanic Verses* are words of the writer which have electrified the society in the same fashion as the words of "reality managers" like Khomeni and Thackarey. But little they realise that writers like Rushdie in their endeavour to deconstruct the society they live in, are the lifeblood of some finest writing today. Gunter Grass's *The Call of the Toad*, a depiction of the post-wall disenchantment and march of the neo-Nazi also faced ban in Germany. Marques in his *One Hundred Years of Solitude* like Grass and Rushdie tries to redeem contemporary man and make sense of a cruel history. But unlike them does not face ban.

Recently, Taslima Nasreen's Lajja also paid for its belief in life; Mani Ratnam for his film "Bombay" faced bans and detestation; all these cases have one thing in common and that is BAN which is an expression of impotency of the banning authority. It would be better to remember creative artists, writers and film makers for their creativity and not controversy.

The Moor's spins around the saga of a Jewish Christian family of multiple stock with mixed heritages. It is a dazzling mix of satire and sadness, history and humour. The novel is set against the drop back of contemporary India. Rushdie gives an expression to his prolonged despair over fast deteriorating social edifice, everything is in mayhem and total anarchy. The historicity and contemporaneity, multi-layers of meanings add motifs to the novel.

As far as major themes are concerned one of course is miscegenation and the other is that of rootlessness—both have their origin and culmination in Moor's plight. Rushdie's characters are of two kinds—main characters and the point of view characters, both are interdependent and have a sort of organic unity. In one of his interviews Rushdie says that the book communicates "a sense of urgency". The narrator is "running out of time, living too fast".[2] This justifies his use of the method of layering. Truth being concealed under the matters as the life is in present day world.

The ban is a curb on the freedom of expression, a censorship on satire but it has failed to make any dent in Rushdie's creativity and sensitive perception of the world he lives in. As he himself said in a seminar on Writers against the State "One of the things a writer is for is to say the unsayable, to speak the unspeakable to ask difficult questions. Everybody has answers. Answers are cheap. Questions are hard to find. If you ask those questions that is a proper function of the Writer". Rushdie seems to be an angry man and his anger culminates in The Moor's Sigh which has defeaning effect.

II

The Moor's is the story of a life-force, a destiny a logic, that shows Bombay in its "....present state of criminalisation and communal disrepair".[3] Rushdie reassembles the story of Moraes Zogoiby from historical bits and pieces which he gathers from Malabar coast to Malabar hill. From Bombay to Benengeli. Moraes says :

> Mine is the story of the fall from grace of a high-born cross-breed : me Moraes Zogoiby, called 'Moor', for most of my life the only male heir to the spice-trade-'n'-big-business crores of the da Gama-Zogoiby dynasty of Cochin, and of my banishment from what I had every right to think of as my natural life by my mother Aurora, nee da Gama, most illustrious of our modern artists, a great beauty who was also the most sharp-tongued woman of her generation 'handing' out the hot stuff to anybody who came within range.
>
> (*The Moor's*, p. 5)

Maternally he belongs to the generation of Vasco da Gama. His Great Grandfather, Francisco da Gama in 1916 joined the Home Rule campaign of Annie Besant and Bal Gangadhar Tilak, and in prison propounded a theory on "The Transformational Fields of Conscience," in which he proposed that each man has spiritual energy similar to electromagnetic field. The theory was extensively criticized. Moraes' Grandfather remained obsessed throughout his life with the Bolshevik Revolution so much so that he would adopt to the leader's image to local needs. His brother was a closet homosexual who named his bull dog as Jawahar Lal, as a protest against imperial loyalty.[4] Moraes' father Abraham Zogoiby deals in underworld activities like trading of girls, explosives and drugs. And with him Rushdie introduces contemporary Bombay full of sound and fury.

A significant role is played by the women in the novel. The Great Grandmother Epifania, a dominating personality who lived during 1877-1938. She fails, in her endeavour to hold the reins of family business after her husband's death. She hands over her business to her younger daughter-in-law Carmen da Gama. Epifania triggered family fued and da Gama business empire disintegrated. Moraes' mother Aurora da Gama's marriage could never get approval from Epifania but Aurora with overwhelming presence kills her :

> Aurora reached the top....saw that "the Chapel doors were open... [She]... crept forward, peered in ... Just then, in complete silence Epifania Menzes da Gama fell sideways and lay still. 'One day you will kill of my heart.' ....that death had been swift and merciful.
>
> (*The Moor's*, p. 63)

Epifania throughout her life left that she was wronged by her husband and grandson Abraham because they could not give her due respect. Her discontentment with life comes in the form of apocalyptic prophecies before her death.

> The concept of "motherness" is looked at from a new perspective. Moraes introspects Motherness— "Excuse me if I underline the point—is a big idea in India, may be our biggest : the land as mother, the mother, as land, the firm ground beneath our feet."
>
> (*The Moor's*, p. 137)

This ironical introspection comes to Moraes on looking at his relatives with Aurora who give him the burden of miscegenation, burden of curses, and uncertainty. Though Rushdie feels that mother-son relationship in a metropolitan is drastically different from a heroic peasant woman image of Mother India. Thus he creates his sort of metropolitan Mother India who could offer nothing but rootlessness to her own son :

> ...Nine months to the day before I arrived, there was a missing night. But innocent—till-proven—otherwise is an excellent rule.
>
> Jawaharlal Nehru was sixty seven years old in 1957, my mother was thirty two. They never met again.....
>
> (*The Moor's,* pp. 177-78)

Uncertainty prevails from the moment of his conception to his birth, his birth has been spectacular, as well as his growth. He among his family members was like a Gulliver who falls headlong into a purgatory authored for him by all those who claimed to have some role in his 'gasping life'.

Moraes is rejected by his mother, goes into exile. He echoes his creator's sadness of exile. Like Rushdie, Moraes is "....as if cast out from paradise.... Displacement was a way for (him) to experience another reality. Another reason is that he should not just stay in the high rise world" but also move in the darker world....[5]

Moor's plight is that he experiences rootlessness and alienation in the society because of its fast changing value system which he is unable to accept, thinks himself to be out of place and out of time.

Moraes grows up in a puralistic society in which his mother (paves) her way to national glory and his father Abraham Zogoiby becomes most influential business tycoon. He also investigates in lives of gallery of rogues : Raman Fielding, an ex-cartoonist, better known as Mainduck, is a leader of regional communal party Mumbai Axis (MA) and has ambitious plans to convert India into a Hindu Rashtra. He conquers the people with his fiery speeches.

It is here in the book that Rushdie's brilliance to have etched caricature that many believe to be of Shive Sena Chief Bal Thackeray, which provoked the leader to give his verdict to restrain the book to enter his domain—Bombay.

Thus, Rushdie does not only ridicules the India, that Nehru brought into being but actually laments the damage done to the vision in the succeeding years. He zooms in on the apocalyptic days : the post Ayodhya, Bombay bomb blasts, India's capacity to consume the news of Rajiv Gandhi's assassination and feels life in metropolis is beyond repair as it is controlled by the underworld dons and white clad politicians sometimes, in nexus with each other and at times in rivalry. In contrast to all this Rushdie also mentions Miss India becomes Miss

World—becomes—the Helen—of—Troy of the Bombay dons who spread their tentacles around her.

III

Aurora Zogoiby, Moor's mother, deals with the literal palimpsests. Her paintings reveal spirit of the age, intense passion and sacrifice. She also paints the vilest of Bombay's villains, as another painting is painted by her protege-turned inquisitor-Vasco Miranda that conceals her image. It is interesting to notice that Moraes undertakes a long journey from Bombay to Benengeli in Spain in search of the mysterious missing portrait of his mother. The painting has autobiographical element of Rushdie's real life. He says :

> "... Krishen Khanna, the painter told me that when he was very young some 50 years ago, he painted my mother's portrait and my father refused to buy it. I think he thought it was too sensual. Khanna left it in M.F. Hussain's Studio. And at some point Hussain painted another picture on top of my mother's portrait and that painting was sold.... The image of that lost painting has stayed .... There is no other sense in which Aurora is my mother."[6]

The missing painting has fitted into the texture of the novel's theme of layered reality it acts like an inspiring palimpsest. Rushdie also considers that Bombay offers palimpsest life to the people :

> The city itself, perhaps the whole country, was a palimpsest, Under World beneath Over World, black market beneath white when the whole life was like this, when an invisible reality moved phantomrise beneath a visible fiction, subverting all its meanings.... How could any of us have escaped that deadly layering?... How could we have failed to be grotesque?
>
> (*The Moor's*, pp. 184-85)

The motif of palimpsest plays important role in Moor's life especially when his love's labour is lost in his affairs with Uma Saraswati and Nadia Wadia. It also indicates the writer's lament about the pointlessness of art in the face of the invisible reality subverting all its meanings.

"Love is one of the greatest victims of this subversion of meanings"[7]. Rushdie explores the outer world of his characters. This provides "great compression and intensity", as he has a large canvas and a large cast of characters and a large number of incidents, thus "the idea of layering, in the world hidden underneath other worlds" acts as the method of writing the novel.

IV

The blurb on the inner flap of the book claims :

> "Surpassing even the imaginative brilliance of *Midnight's Children, The Moor's Last Sigh* is spectacularly ambitious, funny. Satirical and compassionate. It is a love song to a vanishing world, but also its last hurrah."

Rushdie has travelled a long way from his, *Midnight's Children* as far as his imagination is concerned; he has also attained maturity and brilliance which makes *The Moor's Last Sigh* "spectacularly ambitious." Another remarkable feature is that it testifies his "imaginative brilliance" because no other writer has ever thought of reconstructing a family saga of four generations in a compact manner. If on one hand like Marquez (in *One Hundred Years of Solitude*) Rushdie draws on life and times of generations of a family on the other hand unlike him does not refer to solitude of generations but introduces wide range of exciting, thrilling and gasping solution related to the Moor's ..."extensive travelling, maternal curses, the epidemic love and betrayals, of rites and passions and dance of death"? The saga revolves around the cross breed of a Jewish Christian family. The narrator cherishes his inheritance and introduces himself as someone who is neither a Catholic nor a Jew, both or nothing.[8] Below this lies another story of India's reality which is "so plural and so shifting". Rushdie focusses on identity markers like caste, religion, language or place or community. Though, now these roots have been uprooted and call in for redefinition.

Rushdie too believes, satire is the soul of good literature. The book has several rib-tickling passages revealing spoonerism and malapropism. He has preferred his prose with Hindi words metaphorically : the comptrollers in a Kerala spice company are called Mr. Elaichipillai Kalonjee,

Mr. V.S. Mirchandalchini and Mr. Karipattam Tejpattam.[9]

Then there is a pseudo-Bharat Goddess (Mother India) called Aurora. Rushdie spares no opportunity to expose linguistic snobbery often seen among educated Indians to prove their superiority over their fellow country-men.

Thus, *The Moor's Last Sigh* is a satirical criticism of life which is a worthwhile creative endeavour. The State or any political leader has no right to infringe on the right to freedom of expression. Instead they should give Rushdie a 'poetic licence' to think on his line of argument and express. Something which should be viewed critically and objectively rather than subjectively. What though even if it raises a bit of controversy?

REFERENCES AND NOTES

1. S. Parasannarajan, "Who's Afraid of Rushdie?" *Indian Express* 23, Aug. '95, 6.
2. L.K. Sharma, "To Feel Exiled By India Is a Harsh Thing For Me", An Interview, *The Times of India*, New Delhi, Sept. 9, 1995, 14.
3. Sanjay Iyer, "The Palimpsest of Life", *Indian Review of Books*, Vol. V, No. 1 (68-69).
4. Amrit Dhillon, "I Am Pessimistic About the changes occurring in India", An Interview, *India Today*, Sept. 30, 1995 (100-103).

   Rushdie clarifies, "This not a novel that sets out to ridicule India that Nehru brought into being, but actually to lament the damage done to the vision of India in the succeeding years.... Most leading characters are in favour of independence except one....who in order to annoy his family name his dog Jawahar Lal.
5. S. Parasannarajan, "The Last Salaam", *Indian Express*, Express Magazine, 20 Aug. 1995, (1).
6. L.K. sharma, *Op. cit.*
7. Sanjay Iyer, *Op. cit.*
8. L.K. Sharma, *Op. cit.*
9. P. Lal, "Salman The Magnificent", *India Book Chronicle*, Vol. XX, Nos. 10 and 11, Oct.-Nov. '95 (5-8).

11

Fiction as Philosophy : Subversive Strategies in Shivarama Karanth's *Mookajji's Visions*

DR. M. RAJESHWAR
Lecturer
Department of English,
Kakatiya University, Warangal

Shivarama Karanth is known outside Karnataka only as the 1977 Jnanapith laureate and as the author of *Chomana Dudi* (Choma's Drum) which has been translated into English and made into an award winning film. *Mookajjiya Kanasugalu* (Mookajji's Visions) which won for him the Jnanapith Award and which has since been translated into English has not received the critical acclaim it deserves, at least not in English.

Karanth is not just a literary artist. He is also a practising philosopher and social activist and has wide ranging concerns and interests. All through his long life, and he is 95 now, he has enjoyed the image of a debunker of uncritically held myths. He has always been at the storm-centre of social, political and literary movements and has taken an active part in debates concerning these fields. What characterizes his public image is his anger at and impatience with the perpetrators of injustice and upholders of religious dogmas, hegemonistic traditions, oppressive social structures and irrational and dated values and systems. He does not stop merely at registering his protest in the books he writes. His public awareness programme using such traditional art forms as *Yaksagana*, his innovative educational experiments and his active participation in agitations and demonstrations for some public cause or the other show how he tries to actualize the philosophy he preaches.

On a close reading of his works one gets the feeling that Karanth frequently subordinates his artistic and aesthetic achievements to social and philosophical concerns. Starting with *Sameekshe,* through *Alidamele*, and beyond he consistently treated philosophical issues facing mankind. This philosophical enquiry into life often results in a diminished interest in the individual vicissitudes of his characters. G.H. Nayak is provoked to observe in this regard that "Situations never arise in the novels of Karanth which have the capability to...seriously challenge positions taken by the intellectual protagonists. So there is hardly any occasion for Karanth, the artist, to face up to profoundly trying challenges."[1] But then, characterization is not Karanth's forte. Fiction is philosophy for him.

Technically Karanth belongs to the Navodaya School of Kannada writers that includes Kuvempu, Ravabahadur and Sriranga. He shares with them a humanistic and secular outlook, an abiding interest in the life of common man and a zeal to experiment in terms of technique. He, however, differs with them when it comes to glorifying our past. He is basically an agnostic-humanist and realist who refuses, as L.S. Seshagiri Rao puts it, to "idealize or romanticize human nature. There is a compassion in his visions of human life but it is so blended with reflection and assessment that it never grows maudlin or sentimental."[2] While professing an unshakeable faith in the meaningfulness of life, he, along with Kailasam, Sriranga and Adiga laughs "at our colossal ignorance and superstition," exposes "the hypocrisy of our daily lives, the hollowness of our pretensions and the vulnerability of our social, political and religious institutions" and reveals "the core of tenderness, goodness, or sweet reasonableness that may lie imbedded, whether in a traditional or in an unconventional personality."[3]

Mookajji's Visions epitomises the philosophy of Karanth. It is basically a subversive text and it deeply disturbs us. By employing various literary and artistic strategies Karanth debunks the many myths that we Indians have been living with. He lays bare, through the device of the visions of an old illiterate woman called Mookajji, the false sense of pride we have in our past. Through these visions he kaleidoscopically presents the lowly origins of human beings, the many struggles (of existence?) we had to fight, the birth of belief systems, religious myths and social institutions, their crystallization into dogmatised and oppressive formulations and their reinforcement over the centuries by the upper class Brahmanical ethos. There is hardly anything to be proud of in our past if we delve into it and see for ourselves with an unprejudiced and unsentimental eye. Our history has been one long nightmare. We are still perpetuating these myths, and as a result, we have not been able to live life meaningfully or cultivate a broad secular and humanistic outlook. There is much hypocrisy, sentimentalism, fanaticism, intolerance and false sense of pride around us. All this is dramatised and artistically presented in the novel. For this purpose Karanth discards the traditional mode of narration. There is no conventional hero and heroine and no story line worth the name. The bulk of the novel is devoted to the presentation of the visions of Mookajji in which the past comes alive and the present gets properly perspectivised.

The technique of an old woman seeing visions is obviously modeled on the common practice in the south Indian villages of "divinely inspired" or "possessed" old women foretelling events or identifying the divine agency who is supposed to be responsible for the illness or misfortune of the seeker. While the practice perpetuates blind beliefs in the villages, Karanth uses it as a fictional technique for intellectually analysing the past and the present. One is also reminded of the "time machine" technique popularized by the science fiction writers because these visions keep taking us back and forth in time, sometimes as far back as the stone age.

Mookajji is a frank, honest and forthright woman. She is unfettered by traditional values and expectations of society. Taboos never restrain her from speaking out her mind. In her eighties now, she still retains a youthful agility of mind and seems to have acquired, paradoxically, some "uncanny" powers such as accurately predicting the future.[4] Her visions are her chief attraction and source of strength. There is nothing that her visions do not reveal either in the remote antiquity or the recent past. It may be somewhat controversial on the part of Karanth to impute so much knowledge to an uneducated village woman. But he always sends Mookajji into a vision when she reveals and discusses the historical processes, the finer points of belief systems, etc., and she hardly remembers what she says during these visions. During some of the post-vision discussions, however, Karanth goes off balance and seems to speak directly to the reader just as he does in a later novel, *Nasta Diggajagalu* (in which the moralist and teacher has the better of the artist in him).

Mookajji and her "grandson" Subbarao form a perfect team. Their village Moodoor presents an ideal background for contemplation on the past and speculation on the present because in the distant past it was the capital of a little kingdom and ruins are to be found everywhere. A short distance away from Moodoor there are the Nagankal caves which once housed the stone age people. Subbarao is a keen student of history and an ardent admirer of Mookajji (who for others is a sharp-tongued and senile granny). He initiates the visions (by usually placing a relic in her hands), contextualises them and comments on them according to his lights.[5] They usually sit on the *aswatha katte*, the bo tree platform, and engage themselves in philosophical enquiry. The symbolism of the bo tree has to be particularly noted. It was while meditating under a bo tree that the Buddha got his enlightenment. Engaged in intellectual discourse, the duo also appear to continue the tradition of the Guru and Sisya of the Upanishadic literature.

The ideas and thoughts on any particular topic are not presented consistently. The thin story line, instead of imposing an order, only seems to intrude into the fine philosophical speculations and at times even irritates the reader. It is perhaps a real tribute to Karanth's creative powers and narrative skill to write an absorbing and interesting novel with only historical and philosophical issues to hinge on.

As Subbarao, the narrator, rightly understands early in the novel, the visions and tales of Mookajji have the potential to "beat hollow the many mythological stories"[6] that we have known and valued for generations. God and sex are two concepts around which many myths have been woven and many hypocritical practices have evolved. Although Mookajji does not profess to be an atheist, she has a clear perspective on God. She thinks that "since the creation of man on earth, people have joined together in creating a god for themselves" (28). We "ask Him ever so many questions and then we ourselves begin to answer them" (28-29). We do not know anything about Him but we "pretend we do" (29) and "What He means" is invariably what "we feel about it" (29). She then turns her attention to the origin of the many Hindu deities. Shiva can be traced back to the time when the primitive wondered about creation—the birth of children. He thought the phallus—the male genital—and the female counter-part of it, are divine objects since they facilitated creation. They then began to worship especially the phallus—the Siva Linga. Mookajji thinks : "Creation became possible with male and female principles. Human beings thought God created all things in the same fashion" (92). She therefore feels wonder and not shame at the process of creation. In a vision she sees a big number of young men and women copulating around the figure of a phallus. These people are, according to Mookajji, playing the game of creation. There is nothing obscene about it. In fact, Mookajji reads "a sort of reverence for the thing they are doing" (93) and this reverence draws forth the comment : "To be born is no ugly thing; to live is not ugly; death too, is not ugly. Should creation alone be ugly?" (93). Well, for those of us governed by a false sense of values it does look ugly.

As civilization progressed newer and better dressed gods came into existence. There have been hundreds of thousands of them. In fact, there was a time when gods outnumbered men and the avatara theory was erected to solve the problem. The avatara theory identified certain important gods and separate worship was offered to them. The avatars simply "don't make sense" (117) to Mookajji. The avatars have a basically psychological origin. We want "some faith to sustain us in this miserable existence" and we "desire that the wicked should die and the good survive" (191). It is thus that we "bestowed rebirths on the gods. It is our minds that do it" (211). While elsewhere on the globe, especially in the Judaic-Christian world, the many gods and goddesses have been swept off board and the oneness of God has been firmly established, the Hindus, belonging as they do to the only surviving naturally evolved major religion of the world, continue to believe in a multiplicity of gods and goddesses and keep adding new ones every now and then. There has never been anything permanent about these gods. The older Vedic gods—Indra, Varuna, Agni, Mitra, etc.—suffered a diminished popularity and importance and their place has been taken by newly created gods. Gods live only as long as men wish them to live.

Closely allied to God(s) are the religious myths. Freud opined that myths have a purely earthly origin. They are then raised to heavenly heights. Mookajji has similar views. Vaikunta and Kailasa and other divine abodes have sprung from the human imagination. Having created gods men needed to house them so that gods can call them to their abodes and they have to beg for admission. Mookajji observes : "All these are foolish ideas. These are desires we have created for ourselves" and then she questions, "when we say we should not have attachments and desires, how can the attraction of Vaikunta be right, and that of the earth wrong?" (197).

There appears to be an ulterior political motive in the creation of myths. During the time when Buddhism, Jainism, the debased Shaktas and other Shramanic religious traditions and the mainstream Brahmanical Hinduism were vying with each other for consolidation of power, many myths were created to "establish the superiority of their own gods [the Buddha was soon made a god] and to degrade others. They elevated their own deities to great heights and hurled others to the lowest depths. They made the gods of other religions the door-keepers of their deities and temples!" (200).

The mythicized part of the *Ramayana* and the *Mahabharata* does not carry conviction. Mookajji hints at the possible tribal origin of the Rama myth in one of her early visions. She now educates Subbarao on both the epics : "What I believe are a few sober statements the works contain. Like Rama and Krishna ever so many gods were created...I have been so often telling you that if a god really has power he needs no incarnation. All these legends are like the fictitious ghosts that we create for children" (21). The *Gita* which has always characterized the intellectual and religious life of the Hindus, too does not escape critical scrutiny. To her the *Gita* appears to be a bundle of contradictions authored by ten different people and attributed to one mythical Krishna. The very thought that the long sermon was preached by Krishna after the signal for the war had been given is revolting. Krishna makes many contradictory statements during his discourse. He exhorts Arjuna not to yearn for the fruits of his action but he promises that if he is killed in the battle he will be rewarded with heaven. He states that the body is an illusion but orders Arjuna to destroy the bodies of his enemies. He declares that nothing can stain the soul but threatens Arjuna that if he does not fight the enemy he will suffer ignominy. This is mere jugglery of words. The multiple human authors who probably interpolated the *Gita* into the *Mahabharata* had an obvious ulterior motive. They wanted to trick the people into believing falsities by thrusting "their ideas into the throats of their gods" and by seeing to it that "they were spewed out on mankind" (254).

Relevant to God and religious myths is the concept of renunciation. Mookajji is amused and angered by the idea of renunciation. Early in the novel she cites the example of ascetics who forsook their wives and children and went into the forest to do tapasya and to attain to the presence of either Siva or Narayana. These same gods are supposed to be enjoying life with their wives in Kailasa and Vaikunta respectively. How can they possibly bestow deliverance upon the devotees, when they themselves have to find deliverance from their wives? Yet, to continue to think that these gods are real and are capable of delivering mankind is the real illusion. Man never seems to overcome illusion.

Meditation is a fine thing. In fact, Mookajji has been doing precisely that all these years. But to renounce the world and to go to the forest in order to meditate on God is unnecessary. The forest too has its disturbances. Those who go to the forests for doing tapasya are escapists. They are afraid of living with their wives and children because "samsara ...involves us in pain as well as pleasure. They don't want the pain. They don't want sorrow; they don't want death but desire eternal bliss!" (64). Like the proverbial millipede, they withdraw into themselves and think that they are safe. It is a pathological attempt on their part to seek the safety of the mother's womb. But what they don't seem to realise is that renunciation is never completely possible because : "Discarding *samsara* is like discarding one's body. So long as the body is attached to us, we cannot discard it (65).

While visualising the story of the girl of a noble family whose husband took to sanyasa and then insisted on her becoming a recluse like him (which is reminiscent of the Buddha's renunciation) Mookajji observes that " 'vairagya' or the dislike of worldly life must come by itself' (247), if it must. She herself has been living like a recluse all these years. Renunciation occasioned by somebody else's advice is a "drilled and regimented renunciation. It originates from the idea that one has to keep oneself away from woman; association with her is considered a bondage" (247). She therefore vehemently objects to Subbarao's relative Anantharaya's preaching renunciation and when he does not mend his ways she humbles him by exposing his homosexual relation with his student Ramadasa.

Evolution and human history come next under scrutiny. In the treatment of these twin themes there is a gradual progression from early stone age period to the prehistoric times and the recent past. Mookajji strikes at the roots of the romantic belief that life in the past was great. Man's past has been a bad enough experience. Subbarao initiates a vision in her by placing a bone he retrieved from the Nagankal caves. She sees in her vision a primitive man clad in tiger skin. He is a faith-healer and priest. A miserable woman brings a small-pox stricken child to him. The man gets possessed and rants, pointing towards a figure on the ground with a magic wand, that the illness would go. He also officiates at a marriage in his role as a priest. A teen-age girl is married to a middle-aged man who already has eight wives. The marriage is publicly consummated. This vision gives us a glimpse of the earliest forms of some of our well-known religious and social institutions. Belief in God is strengthened by man's inability to cope with problems as in the case of the mother of the sick child and atrocities against women have been given social seal in the name of marriage. The perpetrators have always been clever people like the priest or powerful people like the bride-groom.

The relics and curios that Subbarao secures from the caves and disused temples occasion a number of dreams all of which give us an idea of the beginnings of our institutions, practices and beliefs. A stone blade brings up the image of a strong man who wielded it as a weapon and subdued whoever dared oppose him. He succeeded in kidnapping a woman of a different clan and when they attempted to force him into giving her up he defeated them and drove them away. Since then, perhaps, power has been wielded by strong men and women have been treated as property to be won or lost. The broken bits of a sea-shell necklace, when placed in Mookajji's hands, bring forth the story of a black-skinned young man belonging to the "Tiger Clan" (because they worshipped the tiger as a totem and would not kill the tiger for the world) who eloped with a girl belonging to the "Buffalo Clan" (who too had similar reverence for the buffalo). It would have normally led to a big fight but the girl's people acknowledge the superiority of the groom and quietly return. The story leads to the speculation on the part of Mookajji and Subbarao that totem worship might be the reason behind the "clan customs" among the sudras and "gotras" among the upper castes. The two clans mentioned earlier believed that they are the descendants of the tiger and buffalo respectively. This is meaningless. Equally meaningless is the belief of certain royal families that they are the descendants of the sun (Suryavamsi) and the moon (Chandravamsi). The present family names too perhaps have their origin in equally irrational beliefs.

The bronze icon of a nude man, retrieved from a collapsed stone pavilion by Subbarao, draws an interesting story from Mookajji. The icon was in the beginning the image of Vishnu riding Garuda. It was worshipped as God for many years. But the area was conquerred by the Jains. The image was then melted and forged into a nude figure and placed in the pavilion which had since been converted into a Jain shrine. And when the area was once again taken over by foreigners, a religious sect who slept during day and meditated during night, one of them seized the icon and buried it in the pavilion. It is not just the image of God that changed every time political power changed hands, the people too switched their loyalties. It is thus that "No temple is permanent; no god is permanent" (195). Struggle for survival necessitates changing religious affiliations every so often. This perhaps explains the many syncratic traditions of India.

History has been thus replete with instances of great suffering. It is only the "forgetfulness of the race" which has "kept us ignorant of the suffering of ancient times" (249). It has also preserved many "hostile and conflicting ideas and symbols" (249) which have landed us in the present ideological confusion. We have not been able to learn anything from our past. *Mookajji's Visions* underlines the importance of having the right perspective on our past and the need to interpret our present in rational terms. Mookajji perhaps represents our "collective unconscious." She also appears as though a forceful voice has been given to the tree, a mute witness, in Karanth's novel *Ade Ooru Ade Mara*.

The philosophical message implicit in *Mookajji's Visions* is that we need to adopt a commonsense approach to life, shorn of myths, so as to acknowledge with Mookajji that "the purpose of life is to live and enjoy the beauty of creation...live decently for a while, and when the time comes, leave" (40) and conclude with her that we should live "in a way that is congenial to us and to those around...live in such a way as not to harm others. If we can't give happiness to others let us at least not harm them" (198-99). Myths only complicate our lives and alienate us from our fellow men and even from ourselves.

NOTES

1. G.H. Nayak, "Kannada," *Indian Literature Since Independence : A Symposium*, ed. K.R. Srinivasa Iyengar (New Delhi : Sahitya Akademi, 1973), 109.
2. L.S. Seshagiri Rao, "Kannada," *Comparative Indian Literature*, ed. K.M. George (Madras : Kerala Sahitya Akademi and Macmillan, 1984), 638.
3. V.K. Gokak, "Kannada Literature," *Contemporary Indian Literature : A Symposium* (New Delhi : Sahitya Akademi, 1957), 107.
4. Strange as it may sound, Mookajji reminds us of all people, Agatha Christie's 80 year old detective heroine Miss Jane Marple whose reasoning powers and intellect are her great assets. In spite of the limitations of old age, she always finds out the truth and solves mysteries. Mookajji is not only physically and mentally strong but she unravels mysteries albeit through her visions.
5. After most of these sessions Subbarao has his own rather naive versions of the dreams. These are often amusing.
6. Shivarama Karanth, *Mookajji's Visions* (Bangalore : IBM Prakashana, n.d.), 20. Subsequent parenthetical page references are to this edition.

12

Matriarchal Dominance in Toni Morrison's *Sula*

DR. (MRS.) MONIKA GUPTA
Lecturer
Department of English
Modern European and Other Foreign Languages
HNB Garhwal University
Srinagar, U.P.

In Afro-American literature it is observed that historical reasons have necessitated the Afro-American women to emphasise the role of the mother. Most of the Afro-American mothers are first separated from their husbands and later abandoned by them when they go to the North in search of job. In such circumstances the only alternative before Afro-American woman is her children and particularly the daughter with whom she can confide. The daughters in Afro-American tradition know that their mother is the major force behind them, which help them to define themselves to assert their identity and not be consumed by man. Through interaction with her mother the daughter gets a sense as to what she is and what she ought to be. The literature of Afro-American novelists brings out the complexity of mother-daughter relationships with its moments of tension and tranquility, conflict and resolution. As Mari Evans asserts in her *Black Women Writers* : "The black women braved the ideological structures of the sixties and freed themselves from the role assigned to them in the writings of their male counterparts, where depicted as queens and princesses, or as earth mothers and idealised Big Mommas of superhuman wisdom and strength, they were unrecognizable as individuals".[1]

Toni Morrison is one of those modern black novelists who have consistently delineated the effect of racism and poverty which affects the mother-daughter relationships so severely that it continues from one generation to another. Whatever traits a daughter (would be mother) receives or inherits from her mother, she passes it on to her daughter and this forms a sort of chain of mother-daughter relationships. However, this does not imply that daughter looses her individuality completely and merges herself completely into her mother's self; distinguishing marks of one's identity are always present but the difference is of the degree not of the kind : "The mother encourages her daughter to learn how to be alone without being lonely, to love a man and not to be consumed by him. Through her interaction with her mother, the daughter not only gets a sense of what she is but also what she ought to be and ought not to be".[2]

Mothers and daughters have a special relationship in Morrison's *Sula*. In this paper an attempt has been made to explore and analyse at least three major pairs : Eva and Hannah, Hannah and Sula, Helene and Nel, of mothers and daughters which constitute the theme of the novel itself. The contrast between mothers and daughters are striking but similar. In each relationship the mother is passing a deep inherited feature of her own to her daughter. Though it is a generic and universal function of the female to extend some sense of survival to her offspring. Likewise these characters as women are also fulfilling the same function but catch the attention of the reader because of being a black woman, who are forced to fulfil it through absense, negligence, deprivation and sense of insecurity. The mother-daughter relationship is always non-verbal in Morrison's view she is of the opinion that a mother always tries her best to extend and cherishes a child which she always been deprived of. What is different in Morrison that her Mother-Daughter relationship is always damaged by racism and poverty.

Sula explore the mother-daughter experience at the Bottom, equivalent of the middle class, the Wright's Milieu, and in its poorest sector and the household circumstances of the young Eva Peace. The Peace daughters find some way to connect each other to close distance between them that however, vary with the generation and have strong effects. There is a continuity between Eva and her grand-daughter Sula. Eva Peace, the mother of Hannah and grand-mother of Sula is the most authoritative woman. Her house becomes a "fortress for the women of her line".[3] She lives at Bottom, and her house contains all the elements of the larger community; love, hatred, benevolence, lust, duty. She is an archetype of 'great mother' who nourishes and brings up her family with great care and in her own way. She tells her daughter that taking care of child means is a primary concern of a mother. She is the giver of life and if she feels it proper she can also take the life away. She makes a lot of sacrifice for her children and deliberately gets her leg empulated by putting it before a train in order to get insurance money which would enable her to sustain herself and her children. When her son Plum comes back home as a defeated soldier she first cradles him like a child then, when he is sleeping, sprinkle kerosene over him and kills him by setting him on fire. Throughout her life she leads an independent life hating Boy Boy, her husband, though she does not hate other men. She is a determined woman who stays alike for her children. However, she is as much a part of her two children's death as she has been a part of their life. Her claim to protect her "procreative right is emphasised through the extremes she must endure to save her children's lives".[4] The death of her son Plum and her efforts to protect Hannah from fire throws light on the cynic, extremist mother-daughter relationship.

Eva's daughter Hannah is quiet different in her mother-daughter role. Despite having a lot of sacrifice from Eva she never found Eva to be a loving mother. With this experience and feeling she damages Sula's childhood by confessing that although she had the obligatory love of a mother for her child, she "just don't like her".[5] Hannah's sex experience is also not pleasant and so she teaches Sula that "sex is frequent, but otherwise unremarkable".[6] Sula's diversion from domestic ties seems a natural legacy, for like the other Peace women "she simply loved maleness, for its own sake".[7] Indirectly, Hannah has taught Sula that "there was no other within (than self) the (one) could count on".[8] Hannah is married to Rekus who dies after some time after their marriage. After his death she never bothers to remarry and prefer to live as a widow. She through her "sooty" life style, presents before us an unconventional image of womanhood and motherhood. She refuses to live without the support of a man and takes a steady series of lovers, mostly those who are near to her and husbands of her friends. She defies the role as prescribed by the society to her in the circumstances she is living. She does not want to be branded as a typical woman following the prescription of living by the society. Moreover, she leads her life in this manner because she does not want to be possessed by someone. She dies by fire. The irony is that her mother does her best, but fails to protect her from fire. Hannah's teachings are interpreted as a determining factor in Sula's personality formation. The maternal negation and insensitivity is clearly reflected in Sula's behaviour.

Brought up in the company of grandmother like Eva and mother like Hannah, Sula received the obvious traits of their personality and come up with an entirely changed personality in the novel. The dominating features of Eva's personality and the exposure of Hannah's nature find their complete expression through Sula. She, unlike her grandmother, separates herself from the social ties which brings limitations to her life and behaviour. She is a rebel and protested against the existing norms of society. She refuses to marry and make a family. The matriarchal pattern clearly seems as a passage in the case of Peace Daughters. Whereas Nel felt suffocation in the teachings of her mother and frees herself from her mother's dominance and shallow social vision to gain her individuality. There is a definite continuity between Eva and her daughter Hannah. After her husband Rekus death Hannah moves back into Eva's house. Eva's house "to take care of it and her mother for ever".[9] Despite that Hannah may have been in doubt about Eva's feelings for her but Sula clearly understands at the beginning about her Mother's feeling for her. When she overheard that her mother loves her but cannot like her. The rejection is also the rejection of conventional mother's role in the society. Sula never takes her mother's love for granted. Here the continuity between the individuals is confirmed through emphatic understanding. The sex experience of Hannah is not pleasant and reflected in Sula's personality. Sex is frequent for Hannah and so Sula goes to the church scantly dressed and tries to seduce the husbands of Medallion women. Like her mother she pleases someone when she in return gains pleasure. Sula's inclination towards selfhood and her estrangement from the community can be explained in terms of her matriarchal dominance. Her journey toward selfhood makes her alienated, lonely, estrange and an isolated individual. Her "Me-ness" is the Me-ness of Eva who is the dominant figure in the family. Sula, refuses to marry because she does not want any security in the form of husband who is a hurdle in her love. However her relationship with Ajex is somewhat possessive but not positive. Both Sula and Nel never experienced the love of their father in their lives and they both are "daughters of distant mothers and incomprehensible fathers" [10] Like the childhood their adult life is also influenced by their maternal inheritances. They are inacting to an extent the meaning of adult womenhood explained by their mothers. Although Nel rejects her mother's affection and suffered by the disreputable grandmother but she follows her mother into conventionality. Nel's wedding to Jude is the only way out which can be "thought and done in this world".[11] Sula also followed her mother in her personal life and she could easily discard new sexual partners without involving herself into the love of any man. Following the strong matriarchal connection Nel merges with the community and Sula separates herself from it. Susan Blake rightly says that "the reader never knows quite what to think" of character and events in *Sula*. "Whether to applaud Eva's sacrifice or deplore her tyranny, whether to admire Sula's freedom or condemn her heartlessness".[12]

Sula's life cannot be said a successful one. Her chaotic way of life pursues her own way to freedom but after a long absense of ten long years when she returns to Medallion and completes a cycle of mother-daughter relationship. With Eva she argues with her that "I don't want to make somebody else. I want to make myself".[13]

The individual like Sula has no one to pass on her fierce spirit and she is deprived of the relation of being a mother. She is an individual who attains rare kind of individuality among the other female characters portrayed by Toni Morrison. Her death is a symbol of big pause and a sterility in the mother-daughter relationship. Although she is proud of what she is even of her lonely and dejected condition but she is a lonely empty shell who cannot be explained and measured in terms of a successful strong individual.

Parallel to women of Peace family Morrison has presented Rochelle, Helene Wright and Nel in a different way. Rochelle is a prostitute, an eve and regarded as a dirty woman even by her mother. To save her grand-daughter Helene from any obnoxious influence takes Helene away from her. Morrison has not described in the novel much about Rochelle's way of leading life, perhaps because, she presumes the reader can easily conjecture about it just by the scanty information about her, she gives to them. One can imagine that prostitution as social evil so, those like Rochelle who are a party to it are against the established norms of the society.

Rochelle's daughter Helene has carefully been taught to hate her own mother. She was bought up by her grandmother "under the dolesome eyes of a multicolored Virgin Mary, counselling her to be constantly on guard for any sign of her mother's wild blood".[14] Helene's grandmother made her a productive member of the society. She is married to Willey Wright who has been a seaman. After their marriage Helene comes to Medallion and lives in the lovely house of her husband. She is only firm and a well disciplined woman. She is capable of maintaining balance in the family as well as manipulating her daughter and husband. She knows well how to tackle the ordinary and common problems that one comes across everyday in life. She leads a social and familiar life and fortunately enough she does not suffer any deep frustration and disappointment. However, her peace is at the cost of the loss of her own mother Rochelle. When she takes her ten years old daughter Nel to bury her "pious" grandmother on the way, Nel meets her own still beautiful grandmother. But Helene overlooks her mother Rochelle and makers her realise that she does not want to have anything to do with her. Rochelle accepts this and leaves them but not without a tight, hard, anguished final embrace of her great granddaughter Nel. This first and last embrace is an "emblem of great loss".[15] It also symbolises the separatism among women caused by "polarized and largely Christian Male created images of the feminine".[16] The meeting of Nel and Rochelle is a symbol of the continuity of womanhood and the rude behaviour or Helene shows the loss of the roots of womanhood. Contrary to the teachings of Hannah to her daughter Sula, Helene teaches Nel the politeness, neatness, cleanliness, obedience and hard work. From the social angle Helene may does the right thing but not necessarily good thing in teaching Nel to be "obedient and polite. Any enthusiasms that little Nel showed were calmed by the mother until she drove her daughter's imagination underground".[17] Though Nel's hatred for the oppressive neatness of her home, is a big challenge and a cause of disappointment for Helene, who is an epitome of an ideal womanhood. She has been taught to live a life of puritan.

Helene's daughter Nel has also inherited traits of her mother and she enjoys domestic bliss with her husband Jude. However she frees herself from her mother's dominance and shallow social vision to gain her identity. She prefers :

> "Sula's woolly house, where a pot of something was always cooking on the stove; where the mother Hannah, never scolded or gave directions; where all sorts of people dropped in; where newspapers were stacked in the hallway, and dirty dishes left for hours at a time in the sink, and where a one-legged grandmother named Eva handed you goobers from deep inside her pockets or read you a dream".[18]

Though the novel is after the name of Sula but in fact the novel finally revolves round Nel. The suppression on her part is more intense since she carries the additional burden of shadow that white culture projects into black people. The oppressive is greater than the reactionary. Her motherhood suffers from "an Eve/Mary bedrock of feminine duality, the whore/Madona polarity".[19]

Helene repressed the multi-development of Nel's personality and despite her struggle she could not emerge as a positive female protagonist in the novel. The basic principle of feminity are deeply rooted in Nel's background and arranged systematically, orderly and well contained. But it is a striking note that despite having such a disciplined background she like Sula's disorderly households and always fascinated by her life style. Her mother Helene Channellises Nel's sexual life out of the fear of her own mother's outlaw sexuality. This controlling repression of Nel's sexuality is another angle of mother-daughter experience. The role of men in the life, of Nel is also relevant in shaping her personality. Her father Willy Wright is an escapist husband and a father who never concentrated on the multifascit development of her daughter Nel. She is married to Jude who is not initially interested in marrying her. Jude is a waiter in a hotel in Medallion. She marries Jude not out of love but because they have common need for security. She feels herself worth in accepting the normal societal restriction but she is unable to win the, unlike her mother, the faith and love of her husband. Her husband Jude who develops critical relationship with her friend Sula. Through Nel, Morrison has made an attempt to highlight the disappointment and anguish of a defeated wife. Without Jude she is not able to anticipate life with joy. He betrays Nel and she ends up as sole parent by cleaning houses to support her three children.

After evaluating the two Afro-American families who are suffering with the problem of classism, sexism and racism reveals that mother plays a very dominant role in the shaping or moulding the personality of their daughters and their dormant feelings finds full exposure through them.

Most of the female protagonists of Morrison's *Sula* reject "the tradition of black Maternal world, and Earth Mother".[20] They take it as a myth and not as a reality. Even the traditional women in the novel are crying for liberation and if it is not possible for them they silently pass it to their daughters. The "Black Mother is no longer superhuman".[21] The tradition of contemporary black women's writing defines itself as a "daughterly tradition in relation to a complicated maternal past".[22] The black mother teaches their daughters that how to survive in a racist and sexist world. The cycle of mother-daughter relationship can be analysed in the traditional concept of African families in which the prayers are for the "living those yet to be born and the departed", to neglect the spirits of any of them would "upset the harmony of life".[23]

In this way Eva is alive in the life of Sula and Helene is visible in the personality of Nel.

REFERENCES

1. Mari Evans, 'Preface'. *Black Women Writers (1950-1980). A Critical Evaluation* (New York : Anchor, 1984), p. XXIV.
2. Uma Alladi, Mother-Daughter Relationship in the Novels of Contemporary Afro-American Writer, *Indian Journal of American Studies*, Vol. 16, No. 1, 1986, p. 102.
3. Karla, F.C., Holloway and Stephanie D., *New Dimensions of Spirituality : A Biracial and Bicultural Reading of the Novels of Toni Morrison*. Greenwood Press. New York, 1987, p. 55.
4. *Ibid.*, p. 24.
5. Toni Morrison, *Sula* (New York : Signet), 1973, p. 78.
6. *Ibid.*, p. 62.
7. *Ibid.*, p. 59.
8. *Ibid.*, p. 153.
9. *Ibid.*, p. 59.
10. *Ibid.*, p. 72.
11. *Ibid.*, p. 106.
12. Susan Blake, "Toni Morrison" In Dictionary of Literary Biography (Detroit : Gale Research Co., 1984), p. 191.
13. *Sula, op. cit.*, p. 121.
14. *Ibid.*, p. 29.
15. Karla, F.C., Holloway and Stephanie D., *op. cit.*, p. 53.
16. *Ibid.*, p. 53.
17. *Sula, op. cit.*, p. 30.
18. *Ibid.*, 44.
19. Karla, F.C., Holloway and Stephanie D., *op. cit.*, p. 53.
20. *Ibid.*, p. 26.
21. Uma Alladi, *op. cit.*, p. 102.
22. Marianne Hirsch in "*Toni Morrison : Critical Perspective Past and Present*, ed. Henry Louis Gates Jr., and K.A. Appiah (New York : Amistad, 1993), p. 265.
23. John Mbiti, *The Prayers of African Religion* (Maryknoll, New York : Orbes Books, 1975), p. 102.